Losing My Mind, Mindfully

A 10-Year Journey Through Meditation Practices

To Niamh
Grá agus ádh leat.
Róisín x

Róisín Erskine

First Published in 2025 by Róisín Erskine
with Russell-Alexander Publishing Ltd
Edited by Russell-Alexander Publishing Ltd

Cover Design by

ISBN: 978-1-66641-315-1

Contents

For Egan, you can do anything.

You are loved beyond measure.

Foreword

"Losing My Mind, Mindfully" isn't just a book for the spiritual seeker, and one doesn't have to be a spiritual seeker to benefit from it.

Róisín's journey is nothing short of amazing and one that only a brave heart would embark on. With stories woven together over a ten-year period, this book makes for an interesting read, but more importantly, it serves as a practical and pragmatic tool to inspire and invigorate.

Róisín shares little gems of insight and wisdom alongside simple, accessible guidance that the reader can explore and apply, not only to alleviate symptoms such as pain, anxiety, and panic but also to challenge us to think and live differently."

Marie Quail

Acknowledgements

This book has been in draft format for too many years. I am delighted to finally share some honest, encouraging stories about my meditation journey, hoping to embolden you to persist on your path of self-discovery and authentic living.

Many people have helped me get to this point.

Firstly, I would like to thank my husband, James, who is lovingly referred to as "Skinner" throughout this book. His tireless support, unconditional love, and dedication have made me believe I can do anything. As it turns out, I have yet to prove him wrong!

Many friends and family have been mentioned in these stories; some have been named, and others have not. I'm blessed to be surrounded by people who encourage my curiosity, embrace my weirdness and celebrate my ambition.

Eternal gratitude to Marie Quail, both for her illuminating instruction and support over the years and for writing the foreword for this book. It is a deep privilege and honour to receive such heartening words of recommendation from your teacher.

To all my incredible teachers over the years who have shared insights that only come from a lifetime's experience and wisdom, I am so grateful to have had your company on this journey. Thank you.

To Jenny (Poi) Warnock, I would have never taken the first step without your encouragement, empathetic interview skills and editorial talent. Thanks for helping me nail the first and possibly the most challenging story.

Thank you to Sinéad and Shanti, who helped me release one of the stories contained herein.

Special thanks to Charley for all the time and passion you gave to this, and to all the early readers for their cheerleading and support!

To Jamie Catto, for a kind but direct smack on the nose to tidy up the early passages. It wasn't the feedback I wanted, but it was definitely the feedback I needed to hear!

To June Russell-Alexander, of Russell-Alexander Publishing, for editing, formatting and working with me to bring this book to publication in a very brief timeframe. Her professionalism and knowledge were invaluable, matched only by her generosity in kind while I worked to secure funding.

To my cover designer, Colin Slack, for his expertise, mock-ups, and tireless patience in getting 'the right' cover for me.

Finally, thanks to both my business mentor Patricia Owens at Full Circle and the Newry Mourne & Down Council, through the Go Succeed Business Programme, for granting me the funds to have my manuscript professionally edited and prepared for self-publication including contributions towards marketing.

A Word from the Author

Writing this book has been a massive ambition of mine for quite some time. It has prompted me to reflect on my life's journey thus far and recognise the amazing transformations that I have experienced. It has been about consolidation and integration. All too often in life, we inch our way towards something, and once we finally get there, we fail to recognise the distance travelled, so incremental and subtle the shifts have been when spread over many hours, days, weeks and years. If you can't remember the last time you stopped to take stock of how far you've come, I invite you to take a moment and do that now before you go any further, remembering to give gratitude where possible for making it this far.

What follows is my meandering tale of how I became a trauma-informed Sound and Yoga Therapist and a Therapeutic Martial Arts Instructor. It is underscored by a potted history of segments of my life through which I've transitioned, each cracking open a new reality for me.

Through these writings, I have revelled in the apparent duality of deliciously complementary contradiction. Spoiler alert: there is no correct answer; only each breath, in each moment. You've got to feel it and be with it.

As the title suggests, in this book, you will join me in questioning the nature of reality, our hopes and the expectations that we attach to life events during our personal quest to love, to be loved, and to make sense of an otherwise insanely circumstantial existence.

As I await a formal clinical diagnosis for ADHD (I didn't believe it was a real thing either at first), at times, I questioned if I would ever be able to write a book and see it through to completion. With my lifelong habit of starting creative projects and not finishing them, I assumed that publishing a book would be beyond my reach. And yet, when working for others, I am a successful event producer and project manager, more than capable of bringing their visions to life – go figure.

It's only really been since becoming a parent, followed by the ensuing lockdowns, that I've come to understand my symptoms fully. Experiences of parenthood have shone a light on all my 'neuro spicy' traits that I thought were normal for everyone. Conversely, during the 2020 – 2021 global pandemic, not having to operate in a world designed for and by neurotypical people allowed me to access a level of rest and downtime that it turns out is necessary for me to recover between social engagements, and which generally isn't available in the frantic pace of the digital age.

A big part of how I'm able to see things differently, my creativity, curiosity, dogged determination, and my ability to problem-solve and hyperfocus when learning new skills comes from my neurodivergent brain. But it's also the reason I'm so susceptible to burnout and people-pleasing. It has motivated me to spend my life studying self-regulation practices, to understand the importance of boundaries, and it's the reason I don't bat an eyelid when taking on a challenge, often described in men as 'risk-taking behaviour.' Indeed, it's this heightened neural sensitivity to non-verbal communication which aids me in my work understanding the effects, impacts and treatments for working with people and their trauma. I struggle to name theorists or remember pieces of research I've learned from, but having consumed whatever learning materials of the moment, my brain works to link together the relevant bits and my picture of the world changes without me being able to indicate where the influences came from.

I'm still learning what ADHD is to me. I suspect an official diagnosis will send me down another rabbit hole of hyperfocus and study to learn all about the particulars of my unique make-up, as there are many ways it can manifest in your life. I look forward to getting a diagnosis because it will let me know myself that much better, and yet I know there are cynics out there, just like I was at the start, who doubt it is even a diagnosable condition.

At 40 years of age, I had to come to terms with the notion that ADHD is described and categorised (arguably wrongly) as a disability. It's rather peculiar at this stage in life to be told you have a disability when it hasn't been mentioned before, and yet, women are so good at masking the symptoms of ADHD that many of my generation only begin to pursue diagnosis after the age of 35. We've been termed 'the lost girls.' I have no doubt in my mind that I will receive a clinical diagnosis eventually (though it's a long wait here sadly). I'm glad therefore, before receiving a diagnosis, that I have a catalogue of successes and achievements I can point to in order to remind myself of how capable I am, because the science says I will have trouble focusing, timekeeping, finishing projects, being easily distracted, feeling overwhelmed, forgetting and misplacing things, and while all of that and more is true, if I didn't know how able I am, faced with this litany of negative symptoms, it would be all too easy to give up before even trying.

I know I will continue to challenge what's possible, even with these symptoms. Let this be your sign if you need one. Pursue the thing you want to do, even if everyone's saying it can't be done. Break the mould. Take up space. Failure is only a stepping stone on the way to success, so long as you keep going.

I should emphasise that the experiences outlined in these stories are how ***I*** have perceived them. They are not a judgement on how anyone else handles life's challenges and are certainly not intended to be a roadmap for how anyone can do things better. We are all unique individuals, and what works for one person won't necessarily be effective for another; such is the nature of the lenses and filters we each accumulate throughout our lifetime.

If at any point in this book, you feel anxious, breathless, or like you've read the same line more than a few times without taking anything in, these are good indicators to take a break and practice some self-regulation techniques. This can be anything from gentle stretching or walking to breathing techniques, depending on what's in your toolkit and available to you in that moment. Please be advised that there are topics contained within this book which you may find triggering, and it is important to notice how you feel when consuming that content. Remember to be kind to yourself and take breaks regularly.

The crux of any mindfulness-based practice is to observe *your* thoughts, breath, and intentions. Our words matter, especially in how we speak to ourselves. I caution against glamourising the pursuit of ‘change’ and ‘transformation’ as that implies that you are not already perfect as you are. Instead, consider that you learn and grow by pursuing the things you enjoy, which make you feel alive and bring value and joy to your life. Change and transformation are byproducts of this pursuit, not the main event.

Chapter One

Living a Tactile Life

I can recall only a handful of examples during my life where I felt like I might pass out from the sheer overwhelm of incoming, multi-sensory bombardment. It wasn't so much from the intensity of physical sensation, such as childbirth or a life-changing injury, but from the short-circuiting of my body-mind connection, brought on by the rampant and relentless danger cues firing in my nervous system.

When my friend Charley, a dead ringer for Oxana from the TV show *Killing Eve*, came at me with a knife in the middle of a pressure circle, I could feel panic setting in, but I didn't understand why. If you're not familiar with the concept of a pressure circle, let me explain. When you learn new skills in a slow, accessible setting, paced for maximum uptake and engagement, it can be easy to think you've nailed it. No further work is required. However, accessing that skill competently while under pressure is different altogether. So, periodically in our martial arts training, we will have pressure circles; it's an opportunity to pressure-test the skills we've learned, be that in a particular weapon or approach or, more broadly in breathwork to regulate the nervous system and muscle tone.

From the outside, it looks wildly intimidating, and if you don't have the proper support and training partners around you, it could quickly end in tears. So, this kind of psychological and physiological arousal works best when it happens in a safe container if it's to bring any therapeutic benefit.

The whole group sits in a circle, and one enters the centre. They are tasked with defending themselves in front of an audience. In some settings, it feels like a gladiator battle in an Amphitheatre! A volunteer, anyone from the group (and you don't get to choose who), steps into the circle and, unless we're training in a specific weapon or martial principle at the time, they are free to use their weapon of choice. It is worth noting at this point that while these are training weapons, there is still considerable potential for injury, i.e. a training knife will look like a knife enough to arouse fear, but it has a blunted edge, so it isn't sharp enough to injure - much. A stick, however, is a stick, and the potential for injury with this weapon is based solely on the intention and skill of the individual wielding it. Once the lead instructor has called time, the defender leaves the circle, and this time, the volunteer assumes the role of defender while another volunteer self-nominates to join them in the centre as their opponent.

Pressure circles are fascinating to watch and participate in. They offer rich insights into your habitual tendencies, frame of mind and, more subtly, the quality of your breath. They illustrate how easily we are influenced by an audience, visually demonstrating degrees of mob mentality. They give people what is often their first explicit and tangible experience of sensing a significant change in atmosphere and intention, so tuned in are they to the non-verbal cues on display.

Each time Charley lunged at me with a swipe of the blade, it felt like being knocked backwards into a wave of confusion, contraction and shut down, leaving me scrambling to find my breath, balance or any glimmer of hope in what was descending into a near-comedically futile attempt at self-defence during a simple (but not easy) training drill.

With every missed opportunity to escape the blade or move to disarm Charley, the muscles around my rib cage and throat squeezed a little tighter. The tension in my body and the fear in my psyche were simultaneously sabotaging me while I tried to manage these attacks. The fact that we were being watched by more than twenty of our peers, each set of eyes locked intently on the action, did not help. If anything, it took me more out of my body and further into my head, which is the worst place to be if you're trying to be creative, access a flow state, or remain calm.

I've experienced something similar in artistic performance and media production circles, specifically being observed while performing. Described as 'red light syndrome,' it's the idea that you can practise your craft as often as you like in private. However, when you hit that *record* button and the red light comes on, your performance capability will diminish temporarily to around 20%. This truly reflects how deeply the skill or principle is integrated within you. You must, therefore, practise far beyond the actual attainment of the skill if you ever want to call upon it in times of pressure and stress.

This was where I first encountered the principle:

"Don't practise until you get it right;
practise until you can't get it wrong."
Vince Lombardi

This principle applies to any skill you want to rely on when everything goes sideways. Knowing how to do something is one thing; being able to do it while distracted, emotional, tired, hungry, hurt, worried, etc., is an entirely different skill set that requires dedicated training.

As I'll explain later, I have struggled to be comfortable and confident in front of a group of people for many years, especially if I sensed that they were assessing and critiquing my performance. So, when I say I was in a *pressure circle*, it's hard to imagine a more intense sense of pressure without the situation being genuinely dangerous or threatening.

As far as my body was concerned, the threat of rejection, ridicule and shame in front of my proverbial village, my chosen allies and my friends was as terrifying as it could get. However, there was something more to it; it was so subtle and could easily have been missed. I caught myself forgetting to breathe. I had experienced performance anxiety before, but this felt so much more intense and was proportionate to the events unfolding before me. I had been in other pressure circles, and they had different flavours, but I hadn't experienced this specific sense of challenge before, and I had never been in a pressure circle with Charley before. I wasn't blacking out, although at times, I felt lost, locked out, and perhaps spaced out. I knew I wasn't consciously in command of my body. Everything Charley did seemed to be at double speed, while everything I tried to do was exhausting, excruciatingly slow and devastatingly ineffective, like trying to move through honey.

Another slash and the training knife hit my body again as I stood frozen to the spot, bringing a new wave of panic, sweat and a barrage of internal, self-deprecating insults, connecting the growing lump in my throat to the knotted pit of judgement in my gut. I had lost all sense of time and could easily have believed I'd been entrenched in this scenario for days. Was I going to be stuck in this loop until the instructor called time? When I became aware of this low-key, mental pity party, as I had all but given up on myself, I tapped into what I knew, what I could control. I gently shook my limbs while sighing loudly to discharge some accumulated stress.

During the next attack, I just about managed to dodge the blade. As we passed each other, I landed my first strike, generating a gorgeously satisfying 'thud-ump' deep into her hamstring. When I looked around, she was trying to shake off a dead leg, and I breathed in some momentary relief. Although only lasting for three minutes, this bout of attack and defence seemed to go on for an eternity, and the same question came to mind throughout: "Why is it so much scarier when a woman is the attacker?" A deafening silence echoed in my mind as it scrambled for a rational answer, and in that moment, I realised I was alone. I sensed that no one else in the room felt as I did, or perhaps no one was willing to admit ever having felt this way.

When the challenge ended, Charley and I hugged and laughed, an essential component of co-regulation after such an experience. She remained in the circle awaiting her opportunity to defend, but first, I had to sit before our instructor, still surrounded by the entire training group, for a verbal debrief. There was no hiding how challenging that drill was for me; it was obvious from how breathless I was when I tried to speak afterwards. I gulped in the breaths as I scrambled for coherent thoughts to share, but, at that moment, I could remember very little about what had just happened. Considering that the first time I attempted a pressure circle, I was in a forest and had to walk away from the group to have a quiet panic attack just out of earshot, it felt remarkable that I could sit down without bursting into tears this time. That day, my efforts in the circle might not have looked like much to any spectators. However, for me, this was demonstrable progress, and like many of the battles we each face, the victories fly below the radar and are often celebrated in private.

Clearing away tension and layers of fear opens the door to new insights and more profound understanding; this theme will surface repeatedly throughout these stories. Too often, our own biases cloud our perception. The brain, ever efficient, works to rationalise information and streamline processes, conserving energy for more pressing, one-off events. But beyond that, fear tends to grow stronger with age.

As a child, I loved to ice skate. I would hunker down to pick up speed as I flew across the shiny sheet of frozen fun and crashed into the barriers on either side of the rink. It was my only strategy to stop. I wasn't interested in competing with others; I was content to enjoy the internal experience, the thrill, the chemical buzz, and the novel nature of self-propulsion at such speed.

As I got older and returned to the ice, this time as an adult taking a group of children from the local youth club, I was surprised to realise how much fear I had accumulated. In what felt like a short fifteen years since I had last skated, I had unknowingly magnified the risks in my mind, layering my perception with unevidenced fears about how dangerous it could be. This caught me off guard. After all, I hadn't experienced anything traumatic that might have put me off skating; I had simply stopped doing it. Yet that alone was almost enough to keep me from trying again, despite being a capable, physically literate adult.

When I recognised this in my early twenties, I made a conscious decision to pay close attention to the fears that crept in with age and to challenge some of them deliberately. It was my way of staying connected to my youth, vitality, and sense of adventure and reclaiming a part of my fearless self. Little did I know, it is also a substantial principle within Vipassana meditation: to observe when we react with aversion to something and, instead, to make the conscious choice to practise responding with equanimity, i.e. composed and with a balanced perspective.

I was glad the drill was over, but as I zoned in and out of watching the next pressure circles, that unanswered question continued to niggle at me. I had trained with bigger, rougher guys; some were more skilled, while others were less experienced but, by default, clumsier and, therefore, unintentionally dangerous. So, why did Charley have the capacity to rattle me so much more than any of these other guys? I knew I could leave that question to percolate now that I had identified it, and I didn't think about it again until I found myself facing another younger, arguably more skilled woman with a training knife in class. Her ease with the weapon left me fumbling with nerves, instantly dragging me back to that familiar surge of panic and inadequacy.

A few nights later, it dawned on me. Setting aside the childhood fights with my siblings, the first violent altercation I could remember being in was when I was eleven or twelve years old. Walking back from the local youth club on a dark evening, I heard footsteps running towards me. Suddenly, I was forcefully pushed forward and almost knocked off my feet as someone grabbed a fistful of my hair at the back of my head. I'm sure I froze in a temporary panic as this brute of a pre-teen girl punched me and pushed me around while others looked on. Whatever her intention, it didn't last long, maybe because I didn't act surprised, protest, or try to fight back. I guess it's no fun beating someone up if they don't give you the satisfaction of allowing you to believe that they deserved it. I was used to being trailed around by my hair during fights with my siblings, so I didn't feel in any real physical danger, but I felt ashamed to have been singled out like that. What was wrong with me? Why did I attract this negative attention? Was I fundamentally unlikeable? This event was part of a pattern of hostile encounters that, unfortunately, seemed to come with the territory of attending an all-girls convent high school. I learned early on that trusting other girls wasn't always a sound decision.

Reflecting on my relationships with the opposite sex throughout these stories and how they often sparked revelatory experiences, the men in my life have been the disruptors at various intervals and stages, reflecting my fears, weaknesses and even strengths so that I can see and understand them better. I think it's because, for me, there's less unconscious bias associated with men in the sense of conflict, so the baseline for danger and contention is lower, already making it feel safer to explore difficult themes. In saying that, women have undoubtedly been integral and essential to developing my worldview, but I've come to perceive how they serve an entirely different purpose, for me at least. The women in my life have done more along the lines of providing respite and refuge, and I know that sounds counterintuitive but it's not all women. The circle of trusted women I have gathered around myself have provided the oasis where I could nurture myself back to health, lick my wounds, regroup and rebirth.

For example, one of my favourite things in life is writing. I love sitting down to write or read a letter. While I often send random pieces of mail to various people I adore across the planet, I have one very dear friend, Juliette, to whom I write regularly and have done for years. I really enjoy the tactile act of handwriting. It makes me feel connected to myself, to the physical resources in the moment, and to the intended recipient, no matter how far away they might be. Reaching out to engage with someone so personally generates a tangible warmth in my body. This shared experience of comfort and affection anchors me in the knowledge that even though much time has passed and our lives have taken us in different directions, our friendship still endures. It is timeless, sure and unequivocal, starkly contrasting the vast array of emotions and stimulation we are exposed to in the modern digital and post-truth era. Leaning into all these feelings, taking the time to unpack what something or someone means to me, and learning to trust my body and quiet my mind have all been massively beneficial, but of course, that's not the whole story.

There have been times when these so-called well-being practices, which were supposed to be good for me, felt nothing short of abusive; and times when I've had to circle back because I knew my data was skewed, my perspective was contaminated, and my insights were wildly biased. I couldn't always rely on the feedback loops as they were, at times, so vehemently one-track. So, frequently over the next decade, even though I couldn't explain what I knew or didn't know, I could still say for certain if something *felt right* or not. It turns out that the things I thought were facts were subject to change, and the things I thought were negligible were what I'd been looking for all along.

Learning to trust your gut and recognise when it's just your ego in disguise is a lifelong practice. We're all born with this instinct, yet somehow, we're conditioned out of it. Culturally, we were taught that fact reigns supreme and that only what can be scientifically proven is true. Modern-day discourse is set to eclipse that worldview, where cancel culture (i.e. the deliberate and often aggressive de-platforming of a public figure or contributor) is rampant, regardless of what the facts might actually be. At its worst, it's sustained by quotes and soundbites being taken out of context and moulded to suit a certain narrative. It used to be said that you can manipulate statistics to prove whatever argument you want. With the advent of the internet followed by the arrival of social media, it's now the case that, no matter what you want to believe, you will find all the *evidence* you need to *prove* it online. And don't even get me started on deepfakes.

If I'd known in my adolescence that two things can be true at the same time, that just because someone makes a sound argument doesn't necessarily mean they're right and I'm wrong, that two people can describe the exact same event differently in line with their filters, experiences and even their vocabulary and that neither one is wrong in their perception, I would have experienced much less friction trying to navigate the world. I'd have doubted myself much less and challenged the empty vessels more.

I've never been one for accolades or badges. I don't see myself as competitive, and I don't need external validation to legitimise what I already know. Still, again, this is something I've consciously grown and trained, like a muscle, throughout my twenties so that I could begin to apply it like an innate skill in my thirties. I always had this muscle, but training it allowed me to wield it on command. Now, if I don't like the feel of something, I rarely question why. Sometimes, I'll discover the reason later, but more often than not, I sidestep the extra drama or hassle and move on. I'm past the point of people-pleasing and apologising, and I highly recommend this as a practice worth pursuing.

So, how would someone start this kind of thing as a practice? It begins with becoming aware of where and when you habitually say *sorry*. As is often the case, the word likely falls out of your mouth without any associated meaning, similar to a greeting or other familiar phrase. Once you've clocked your habitual use of the word, notice what happens in your body when you say *sorry*. For me, it's a subtle sensation of collapse: the want to feel smaller, to shrink and withdraw. But often, it's not commensurate to the situations where we typically deploy the word. If you continually apologise for yourself, for existing, breathing and making your way through the world, you are rehearsing a mindset of "I'm not worthy," "I'm lesser than." Your brain believes what you feed it, so this is not a healthy routine to practise.

Be aware of when you typically apologise and choose instead to tune into your breath, gently re-inflate your torso, elongate your spine and take up a little more space in the world. That is how to respond when social conditioning has you believing you should be excusing yourself or saying sorry for simply being.

I appreciate that some people will be incredulous at reading that, and that's okay. I also suggest you reserve your apologies for when they are genuinely required. If I feel like I owe someone an apology, they will get that apology, wholly, sincerely and unreservedly. This alone has been a powerful practice for me. To observe when these feelings of being not good enough come up; to sit with the feelings of discomfort and the fear of rejection; to deliberately cultivate a certainty of self that goes beyond superficial displays within cultural or social constructs in a bid to be regarded as a well-mannered good girl, is an approach that calls for courage, trust, and a level of faith in what's been felt, expressed and known between you and another. It calls for hope that they can lean into what they know to be true and a belief that they will unequivocally afford you the grace of understanding without the need for explanation and love you anyway. If nothing else, it unwittingly roots out those who only seek to engage with you because of what you do for their ego.

To give you a concrete example of how I practise this, many people over the years have benefitted from my unwavering support and generous nature, but these days, I prioritise my family unit. As I see it, my son is hurtling through his younger years at a rate I would have found difficult to believe if I weren't seeing it with my own eyes, and it won't be long until he is a grown, autonomous adult out exploring the world without his parents by his side. I believe I have a finite and ever-shortening time with him, so with each day's passing, I focus a significant amount of my attention on creating good experiences in a loving home for him. A substantial part of that is modelling good digital hygiene. I frequently plug my mobile phone in to charge in a room I know we won't be in. It allows me to connect with him without distraction, untethered from the digital realm.

When I return to my phone, I'll often have received a flurry of notifications, be that email, messages, missed calls, etc. If I am to make this a sustainable practice, I can't simply follow up on all those things as soon as I return to my phone. I can't live my life reacting to when people have decided it suits them to show up in my Inbox with whatever degree of request (and honestly, it could be any number of things). Typically, I'll triage the messages. Urgent stuff gets done first, though not always immediately. Messages that require me to contemplate a topic before I respond, or those that generate conflicting emotions, will be set aside until I feel well enough resourced to deal with them. It could be hours or days, weeks or months before I feel I can respond fully in my own authenticity, as opposed to being reactionary and risk being left with some emotional hangover for responding in a way I might later regret.

Overthinking social situations, ruminating on the things I've said and especially instances that might be perceived as oversharing, are symptoms of my ADHD that generally left me feeling ashamed in the past. Instead, I now choose to communicate at a pace I am comfortable with, and that helps massively.

Object impermanence is also a significant aspect of my ADHD. Sometimes, it is the case that I forgot about the message, the person, the appointment or the plans I agreed to, only to remember (or not) sometimes months or even years later. When those memories return to haunt me, it's easy to end up in another shame-filled spiral. Being unable to manage simple interactions with others can really undermine your confidence and leave you feeling like you've failed at basic human function. It can be chronically devaluing and undoubtedly costs relationships.

Now, I'm not clear what the cut-off time to reply is before you get accused of ghosting or gaslighting someone, and don't get me wrong, they are two very serious words. However, they are often applied liberally to situations that don't necessarily meet the definition. Still, in the event of receiving an unsolicited message which I never reply to, it often comes down to numbers. There are only so many hours in any day; most of mine are already spoken for at this stage. The replies I do send, however, ***never*** start with phrases like, "I'm sorry," "I'm sorry I'm only seeing this now," "Sorry I'm only replying now," or "Sorry, I meant to call you sooner." Nope. These are conscious choices that I'm making or symptoms of my neurological function, and I will not apologise for choosing where I invest my time to comply with convention and rehearse a gender narrative that seeks to keep me obedient any more than I will apologise for the way my brain is wired.

Sometimes, I'll even turn my phone off for an entire week - wild, I know - like when I've gone off into the woods for a training seminar. I appreciate that the world still turns while I've chosen to unplug during that time, but I refuse to return to a backlog, replying to what is now essentially the past. As an individual, you have the right to send whatever you like, and I, as an individual, have the right to prioritise what I respond to within a chosen allocation of time and energy. I cannot give more than I have, and I refuse to burn myself out trying.

I understand that this approach can leave people bewildered when the expectation is that instant communication and connection are available at the drop of a hat. I get that this is not the language of modern-day business, especially for sole traders. I also recognise that this approach means many will think me rude, lazy, difficult and ungrateful. However, it's not my job to conduct my life in a way that is agreeable to others, meets expectations and maintains the status quo. It's my job to live without regret, to honour and love myself. Therefore, for the short time I have in this phase of my life, I am devoted to raising a young family and instilling the tools I know they will need to give them the strength and wisdom to navigate what comes next in this increasingly unstable and unpredictable world.

Beyond that, I work hard to resource myself to be a kind, supportive, and authentic source of strength, comfort and hope for others, but that's on my schedule. I'm not some *on-demand* app. I'm human. Anyone who has spent time with me in person knows I'm there; I'm present and available to connect. I'm not on my phone every five minutes. I'm not sitting with one eye on our conversation and the other on a screen. I treat my phone like an answering machine rather than a direct line, and I don't expect more than that from anyone else.

These days, my boundaries are much clearer than they've ever been, and it's thanks, in part, to developing a strong and robust sense of self and mindfully moderating my language and self-talk, as well as my exposure to other people's projections, fears, and opinions.

Chapter Two

The Buddhism Bit

My primary purpose in life is to alleviate unnecessary suffering for myself and others; a Buddhist concept that has become the thread that runs through all my work and was the heartbeat of my grief story, which unfolds later as a massive part of this journey. Maybe this work resonates so strongly with me because I grew up in a post-conflict society as a member of the "peace generation" in Northern Ireland. Although I was never exposed to the violent conflict first-hand, insofar as my immature consciousness of human development could perceive, it has unequivocally shaped my trajectory since the beginning. I spent my youth observing and turning away from violence, conflict and trauma.

When I was eleven, I decided to become a vegetarian. Since then, I have been unpacking what it means to live a life of nonviolence, intentionally minimising the friction and conflict I create internally and externally.

At the age of twenty-one, I took a 180-degree turn from avoiding conflict, dedicating the next fifteen years to working with perpetrators of violence, conflict and trauma. This enormous shift in perspective ultimately came about after a sequence of seemingly minor events and new interpretations, which led my world as I knew it to unravel, not for the first time and, as would become clear, not for the last time.

By then, I was working full-time in the County Down town of Downpatrick, where I was born and raised. I had fallen into a party lifestyle that was neither sustainable nor, in all honesty, enjoyable. With the cracking open of my previously secure, predictable existence, I observed a distinction between the experience of disruption and conflict; they may appear similar, but ultimately, they are felt and leveraged completely differently.

At this point in my life, I had learned that there is nothing to fear from change. The unknown shouldn't be dismissed in favour of the familiar. So I uprooted my life, left everything I had thought I wanted, and started again from square one. I bowed to every poor decision I had ever made, accepting that the veil had dropped; that what I once placed on a pedestal as my ultimate desires and ambitions were nothing more than trauma bonds and fear responses, longing to belong and aching to be loved.

I moved back into my parents' house, taking a very, let's say, "scenic," unnecessarily long and gruelling way home. There, I got the chance to try new things, make mistakes and fail without the outcome being linked to my financial security and my ability to support myself as an adult. What a huge relief and privilege that was! On reflection, I am convinced that this unconventional path of immersing myself in states and experiences in such stark relief and sharp contrast to my own was the ideal training ground to prepare me for the many challenges I would face on this wild adventure of personal and spiritual development. Later, it allowed me to raft together these converse understandings and to surf the waves of uncertainty and post-traumatic growth.

Bridging the gap between opposing external contexts and internal forces within, required a painstaking process of personal enquiry. One of my key learnings from this process was another Buddhist principle:

"Contemplate impermanence; meditate on the transient nature of reality."
Buddhist Teachings

At twenty-six, I was working on youth projects in post-conflict Northern Ireland. I spent years learning about and implementing the idea of "unconditional positive regard," a central tenet of the ethics of working with young people. Through this work and integration, I came to recognise that I did not have this outlook towards myself, and since then, I vowed to develop my sense of self-compassion.

Around this time, I heard a quote that has stayed with me. It's one I still use when trying to explain to academics the gap between understanding and application of social policy:

"People don't care how much you know until they know how much you care."
President Theodore Roosevelt

This is a very keen observation about the art of human connection and indicates how you might begin to engender trust when working with marginalised individuals and groups. It suggests prioritising which information you share to build rapport.

However, it also has the potential, particularly for those with people-pleasing tendencies, to lead you to think that you must care about everyone all the time. To be considered a good person doing good work, you may feel that you must go above and beyond what is expected. This can lead to self-sacrificing behaviour, leaving little room for self-care, pause and reset, creativity, and authenticity.

I was about seven years into my youth work career, working in areas that ranked in the top 5% of the Multiple Deprivation Indices, which means that I spent most of my time working with children whose parents encouraged them to shoplift, whose community encouraged them to breach the peace and revolt against 'the system,' and whose experience of trauma coupled with a lack of opportunity or resource to heal, led them to addictions and self-medicating; from gambling and poly-drug use to all kinds of high-octane risk-seeking behaviour, an altogether dangerous cocktail which saw many of these young people repeatedly and for some, perpetually entangled within the criminal justice system. I worked with young people who had already written themselves off and were hell-bent on self-sabotage. It was, at times, soul-destroying to learn how some of these young people viewed themselves, their prospects and aspirations.

When I say I was seven years into my youth work career, I was three times beyond the expected burnout timeline of two years for a professional youth worker. When I first heard this statistic, I was floored. How could you burn out from a career quicker than you could qualify to become professionally employed in it? And yet, at this seven-year mark, I knew without any doubt that I was burnt out. I had lost confidence in my capacity to function effectively. Worse yet, I knew I had lost the level of compassion I had embodied since I first encountered the phrase "unconditional positive regard." I could no longer access this perspective easily. This unwritten requirement to care infinitely about everyone and everything coupled with trying to operate in a desperately under-resourced sector, was so unsustainable that it had, over the years, become compassion fatigue. I could see its impact on my work, and I didn't like it.

Around this time, I participated in a vast outdoor performance called "Land of Giants" on the Titanic Slipway at the Belfast Docks. This would become a pivotal moment in my learning about meditation. Still, before we move on to that, I want to share one of the smaller glimmers of realisation of the self that led me to feel like meditation was home by the time I got there.

I wasn't always so keenly aware of my connection to myself, and I was pretty numb to connection with others, something anyone can achieve through distractions and a party lifestyle. I distinctly remember the day I recognised that something would have to change. I was sitting on a bus, making my way home, and as I glanced out the window, I saw a lady who looked outrageously angry and maybe a little bit dangerous. "She'd knock you out!" I thought. In that split second, I realised I was looking at my reflection. I understood then that my demeanour was harsh, aggressive and unwelcoming. I certainly didn't feel as angry as I looked. My embodied state was one of disconnection, disassociation and rejection.

From then on, I decided that any time I noticed my face do the "bitchy resting face," I would flip it and exaggerate it into a smile. Believe it or not, this is something that I would later teach in yoga classes when people were struggling with poses or wrestling with their internal monologues. I trained myself to smile with intention for what felt like years, but gradually, over time, it became easier. Then, it became normal. I began noticing how positively others reacted to how it made them feel. Through this, I learned to be more intuitive and act more intuitively. I soon accessed a new world of connections and opportunities through this enhanced, energetic disposition. I realised that how I showed up in the world, consciously or unconsciously, could drastically impact the quality of my connections.

As humans, we are designed to co-regulate. From the moment we are born, we learn to manage illness, overstimulation, environmental challenges and trauma through co-regulation with our primary caregivers. And it's not something we grow out of; we learn to value it less and less until it pales into insignificance, barely even a memory.

Smiling, vocalising, and *Pranayama* breathing all stimulate the vagus nerve, directly impacting our connection to ourselves and others. The vagus nerve runs from the brain stem, which connects your brain to your spinal cord, and is located at the bottom of the back side of the brain. It runs through your tongue, lower jaw and vocal cords, wrapping around the heart, lungs and diaphragm, ending in the gut; which is why smiling, humming, and breathwork specifically are interventions we can all use to improve our mood and internal landscape, while also enhancing our relationships with others. Since this is the part of the body which is concerned with sensing and processing fear, when we learn to regulate it through such practices, we inevitably become less bound by fears of inadequacy or failure, and we say *yes* to more things we want. It expands our potential for accessing all the gifts that life has to offer.

If we genuinely want to create meaningful connections, we must begin by connecting authentically to the *self*. I have found that singing and smiling regularly are the simplest and most effective ways to do this. I say "simple" because in the earliest days of life, before we were burdened with thoughts of not being enough or the weight of other people's opinions, we all knew how to smile and sing. These things are innate to the human experience.

Back to my introduction to meditation. The North of Ireland, or Northern Ireland if you prefer, has a recent history of violent conflict, and we have been trying to navigate peaceful ways forward for over thirty years since. I participated in a cross-community cultural event as a musician and Streetwise Stilt-walking Samba Band member. We were part of a four-hundred-strong drumming corps made up of all manner and traditions of drummers; we had Bodhrans, Djembes, Dhol drums, Lambeg drums, Timbas, Bongos, Tambourines, Surdos - you name it, we had it.

During one of our rehearsals for the performance on the Titanic Slipway, I spoke candidly to my friend, Marcella. Marcella has a friendly face and oodles of blonde curly hair. She dances to the beat of her own drum, metaphorically and literally. When we were taking part in a rehearsal, she kindly asked how I was doing. I've learned to answer that question honestly, taking time to check in with myself first, then choosing words which accurately reflect my reality and sincerely convey my state.

"I'm tired," I said. "I'm not sure how else to describe it, but I feel a bit undone, you know? Like I'm fraying around the edges. I've never felt like this before."

"Oh," she said, "you need to go and see Sally Taylor. She teaches meditation in her yurt in Saintfield!"

Saintfield was about fifteen minutes from where I lived in rural County Down, and I was surprised to hear about this meditation class. Usually, I'd have to travel to Belfast or abroad to access anything so unconventional; at least, that was the case fifteen years ago! I didn't know what a yurt was, though I took an educated guess. I knew nothing about meditation except for the few guided practices we'd done in school as part of Religious Studies. As for the teacher who taught that subject in our school, let's just say she wasn't my cup of tea. I didn't like her demeanour, I couldn't enjoy her prosody, and I wholeheartedly resented what she was trying to teach. As far as I was concerned, organised religion was the root of all evil, the alleged justification for many wars, and, in its crudest expression, simply an instrument for managing a majority of dumb, gullible people across the globe. However, I believed I was much too smart and sophisticated a critical thinker to fall for this stuff! I had witnessed first-hand the inherent wickedness of organised religion that was rooted in fear, hatred, division and tribalism. Let's face it: this is the context in which I grew up. The generation before me spilt blood over which brand of Christian they were, or so it was conveniently described through the media.

At quite a young age, I rejected all that and instead turned inwards. I became a vegetarian at the age of eleven. This is not unusual in terms of child development stages, as we all explore and refine our understanding of personal ethics and values at around this age. I was the only vegetarian among five children in our family of seven. I remember coming home from school late one winter evening after staying for choir practice. I was sitting at the kitchen table, trying to force myself to eat some steak and kidney pie. As I sat quietly, pushing the gravy-soaked pieces of flesh around my plate, I felt sick in the pit of my stomach. Previously, this meal had been one of my favourite comforting winter meals. And yet, I couldn't get my fork to my mouth through all the awful guilt and heartache of the reality in front of me.

Ethically, I couldn't resolve the taking of a life to gratify some fleeting notion of hunger or taste. I couldn't understand how other people could justify killing an animal solely based on the fact that it tasted good or that they'd always done it. I've been a vegetarian for thirty years and never believed I could be anything else.

I realised pretty early on that I was in the minority at such a tender age to think of and care so deeply for animals that are farmed solely for consumption. I also learned quickly that most people didn't react positively to my interpretations of the subject. Ironically, they were the people who would raise the subject just as we sat down to eat together. I did my best to be gracious and explain that this probably wasn't the time for such a conversation, as I didn't want to put them off their food. And each time, the reaction was surprisingly similar. People generally became quite defensive, if not entirely laser-focused on trying to convince me of the irrationality and idiocy of my seemingly juvenile choice. Perhaps they saw my divergence from the norm as a judgement on them. It wasn't.

It was a position I came to for me and my peace. I couldn't sleep at night knowing that I had influenced, caused and advocated for the desecration of another being. I didn't waste time wondering what other people thought of it. I just knew I couldn't participate. I recognised the distinction between having the stomach for hunting, animal farming or husbandry and not. I slowly worked my way to the understanding that if I wouldn't be able to slaughter and prepare an animal to eat, then I couldn't ethically avail of the option to have someone else do the dirty work whilst I consumed without conscience or consciousness.

I now understand this transition as a period described as Stage One of Meditation, *"The Wake-up."* Stage One is generally characterised by a sense of dissonance, an awareness that things aren't necessarily how you had previously understood them and a realisation that choosing to explore that notion further likely requires a break from the norm, to choose to live differently, deliberately. I had no idea why I was becoming more aware of these things then. It certainly wasn't due to a formal seated meditation practice or contemplating social constructs and the ego. However, having been through these cycles many times, I can see how each near-catastrophic clash with reality has led me to deeper knowing, feeling, and relating. This journey is often hard to articulate but is unequivocally grounded in the inherent wisdom of "It just feels right."

Throughout this book, I describe my understanding of six loose stages of spiritual awakening as I have experienced them. There are as many different descriptions and variations of this as stars in the sky, and they can be as detailed or simple as you like. Some describe them in a different order, using different terminology, or emphasising different aspects; some believe we travel a linear path, going from start to finish only once, while others, and I, would say that we can have cyclical and parallel processes running concurrently and that each cycle brings a new depth of perspective and wisdom. There is no right or wrong to this experience or these descriptions since we all start from a different place, all carrying different "weights" and using different guides. The path will look different for everyone, yet we all pass the same, often predictable landmarks along the way, more or less.

So, when meditation was first suggested to me, and to study with a practising nun no less, I can confidently say that I was sceptical at best. I'd been practising yoga for years on and off but had never formally ventured down the path of meditation. I didn't do any research into this practice, deciding instead to go and see what would unfold. This began a ten-year relationship with mindfulness-based meditation and perhaps my third obvious run-in with a Stage One awakening.

I remember arriving at the address, guided by my Satnav. I had ended up on a single-track road, and I wasn't sure if I was at the right place as it seemed pretty wild, especially in the dark. I remember coming around the corner and seeing a little stone path meandering towards a roundhouse - the yurt. I instantly fell in love with the gently sloping roof, the beautifully colourful, ornately decorated doorway and the exposed wooden structure inside. It was welcoming, cosy and deceptively spacious. As I entered the yurt, I felt some relaxation almost instantly. Despite having never been there before, nor ever having seen anything remotely like it, it felt like home. There was a familiar smell of incense, seasoned timber and vegetable broth. A few people were gathered around a table in the centre of the space, sharing a cup of tea while they waited for others to arrive.

When Sally called time, we were invited to sit and shown to a pile of cushions alongside some tiny wooden stools that looked like picnic benches for teddy bears.

Those little stools were for adults to sit on to meditate. As we prepared for the unknown, I felt anxious and nervous. Part of me was concerned that I was walking straight into a cult; that, having spent years of my life turning away from anything remotely spiritual, I was now willingly walking straight back into some brainwashing camp. I probably wouldn't have stayed if I hadn't been so sure I was already on the wrong path with these frayed sensations. Still, I knew everything I was doing had brought me to this point of unravelling again, and I wasn't too big to admit that I could easily have taken a wrong turn. Later, I understood that this was another key phase of the spiritual awakening process. I'll describe these more as we begin to piece parts of this story together.

We took our seats, and the practice began. I've always been very comfortable sitting on the floor. It's common for those with ADHD to prefer the floor, and it's referred to as "perching." I've done this everywhere, from busy streets and travel hubs to classrooms and conferences. There's a security in being so close to the ground that is difficult to express. So estranged are we from the idea of difference and diversity of behaviours that I have frequently been met with looks of confusion, bemusement and even ridicule for daring to enjoy my preferences for engaging with my environment. I took one soft cushion, placed it under my sit bones and settled into the encroaching silence. We meditated on three prayers during this session, with a short discourse in between. For each one, we were given some context, guided through a practice, and then invited to recite the words on the prayer sheets.

It struck me that actively sending out thoughts of compassion and gratitude was not a part of my religious understanding. I grew up in the church, served on the altar, and sang in the choirs. I participated in the Catholic sacraments, rites of passage and spiritual milestones. I can recite word-for-word the parts in a Mass service where we, as a congregation, express these exact sentiments. Yet, this intention and expression seemed entirely alien to how I had interpreted such practices. This ritual is replicated within the faith in which I was raised, but I guess it was easy to bypass it. For whatever reason, cultivating kindness and praying for others was someone else's job; that was my heavily biased misunderstanding of it at the time.

"Prayer" in the yurt felt different. It was like I was given autonomy and responsibility for ensuring that I contributed to alleviating the suffering of others, and they would never know of it (a familiar sentiment, yes?) I guess that's one thing I've learned repeatedly through years of observation. Often, we can hear, use and even reiterate the same words throughout our lifetime, and then, at some point, the penny drops, something clarifies, and suddenly, it's as though we've heard something for the first time. It reminds me of *Jean Piaget's "Theory of Cognitive Development,"* which outlines how our capacity to perceive and understand things evolves as we age. It describes how we can have all the information we need in front of us but cannot organise it coherently and rationally because we are still limited by the juvenile perspective, which places us at the centre of our understanding and experience. This is known as egocentrism. It's a completely appropriate stage of development for a child; however, it is something we ought to grow out of eventually. So, learning how to receive and process information as a task, independent of egoic influences, is critical to perceiving and realising fundamental principles as an adult.

If you ever feel frustrated on your journey, whether it's spiritual, developmental, learning new skills, or solving problems, because you're being asked to go back to the basics, you're likely missing important insights because you think you already know the material. Egos aside, going back to the basics regularly is where you will find wisdom in abundance. Simplicity and non-judgement are the most frictionless avenues to true peace and contentment.

My understanding of faith-based practices was heavily tainted with fear, mistrust and trauma. I can see how the features and practices described above were present in my frame of reference but distorted through different lenses, and deep down, I saw them as grossly imbued with hypocrisy. When I was growing up, we frequently heard church members on the news broadcasts lambasting the *other* community. I found it difficult to stomach such vitriol and dishonesty, especially when preached by clergymen, "Men of God," supposedly. It's hard to respect adults when, as a child, you feel you are infinitely more mature, reasonable, truthful and compassionate than they are. I found the toxic narrative entirely incompatible with one of my core values, fairness, which is quite heavily and strongly aligned with my commitment to nonviolence. I'm unsure if this prioritisation of fairness is a genetic trait, as it's something I've heard my father express (albeit in other terminology), or if it's an environmental reaction to growing up in a segregated society, or both. It's a recognised characteristic of ADHD and a personality trait of my zodiac sign - Taurus (anyone who knows me doesn't need to be told I am the sign of the bull).

I continued to attend these meditation sessions for a few months, and when we broke for the summer, my relationship with Sally, the Buddhist Nun, ended. The practices, however, were now a part of my life. In those few months, I had learned so much about cultivating my awareness, my inner sense of calm, the frequencies I was emitting, and the intentions behind them, that I couldn't unlive or unlearn them. I studied these sessions with all my senses, observing the rise and fall of my thoughts, physical sensations and preferences. Using these simple practices, I noticed a significant shift in my capacity to decompress from the stresses of everyday life. This mindfulness stuff was pretty effective! This felt sense of proficiency and an ability to access more serene states on demand is indicative of the Second Stage of Meditation, known as the "*Bliss*" stage, for obvious reasons. Letting things go and returning to feelings of connectedness and intuition becomes almost effortless. It feels reassuringly familiar yet stirringly unchartered, full of possibility and potential.

Around this time, I was fortunate to be in the company of another friend and guide. I was explaining some complex critical thinking over a late-night drink in the kitchen, trying to get to the root of these thoughts, when I was offered two books to take home and read. The first was *Scientific Existence of the Proof of God will soon be announced by the White House, by Da Love-Ananda*, and I must admit, the concepts in this book are so dense that, after more than a decade, I'm still not finished reading it. The second book was *Buddhism Without Beliefs by Stephen Batchelor*, and this framing felt much less confrontational to me. So I read it, and then I read it again, and again. This short book used real-life examples to demonstrate a simplified mindfulness-based meditation discourse, highlighting where we can often default to criticism and cynicism in the absence of facts or personal connection. It helped me to understand that many well-being practices with a spiritual aspect can be accessed without having to buy into the accompanying dogma completely. If it wasn't for this book and this most astute friend, who had a copy and knew when to share it, I might have traipsed along the same path for many years; I could still be on it yet! I am most grateful to Mr Fee for having my back and so generously sharing the wisdom and resources he'd gleaned over his lifetime when he could just as easily have left me circling the drain.

"The greatness of a man is not how much wealth he acquires, but in his integrity and his ability to affect those around him positively." Bob Marley

---

The integrity part here is essential. It’s not a man's selfless sacrifice that makes it sustainable and profoundly, authentically human. It's how he can affect change *through* his integrity.

So, I found myself in this bizarre new place of collapse and rebuilding. I didn’t recognise what was happening, but I knew that a shift, a quickening, was occurring. This exploratory philosophical and spiritual mission had taken a new turn, one where I felt like I was in free-fall, battling my demons in an intimate and yet soothingly detached way.

Stage Three of Meditation is one of the most inherently disruptive stages because just when you think you’ve nailed it in Stage Two Bliss, you find yourself completely unable to access the same practices with the same ease, if at all. It can be wildly frustrating and hard not to beat yourself up thinking you’ve done something wrong. In this stage, you enter “The Dark Night;” some call it the “The Dark Night of the Soul” because it can be quite an isolating feeling – almost like you’ve been stranded, alone and in the dark, wondering how you will ever find your way back. For me, it felt like pulling at the end of a thread which threatened to unravel the entire garment, and in so doing, it became irrefutably clear that I could never wear this item again, that time had passed, and yet with this transition, I had an opportunity now to reimagine the garment becoming a much more effective and tailored one. While it’s an experience akin to fumbling around blindly in the dark, this process is actually your redesign phase, where previous constructs are rejected in favour of more appropriate, relevant and comprehensive parameters and perspectives. In short, wading through this testing environment is your first opportunity to develop and/or deepen your sense of faith, which will be tested repeatedly as you progress.

I would say that now, I've come to a point in my own practice where I don't consider enlightenment to be this shiny-haloed experience of infallibility and serenity. Instead, I see it more like clearing out that old junk drawer we all have, taking time to go through and sort each of the pieces, discarding what is no longer of use, measuring the sentimental value we apportion to otherwise worthless items, and re-ordering things that we will need easy access to as a priority. It's a job that always takes longer than you anticipate. You'll likely stumble across things you didn't realise you were still holding on to, and there's every chance you'll find something that packs a substantial emotional punch, which sends you reeling and takes a bit of time to recover from.

Often in this stage, you'll uncover aspects of shadow, and when you articulate them, your peers or family might remark that you don't sound like your usual optimistic self. Like learning to balance, the journey towards enlightenment or freedom is a constant work in progress. You'll veer to one side of the middle and then the other as you seek to maintain equilibrium. And as with everything else in life, it is a *use it or lose it* kind of deal.

If, like me, you choose to take the path to liberation from suffering, or 'enlightenment' as it's more frequently termed, you will likely experience not only moments of ecstatic joy and soul-stirring clarity as you realise just what's important in life and how much influence you really have over your state of wellbeing, but you'll also encounter new depths of doubt, fear and friction because it doesn't just change how you see the world outside, it requires you to do a deep and honest self-audit of your behaviours, motivators and internal monologue. However, as I have learned repeatedly through meditation, the deeper I enquire, the more I see the same patterns repeated infinitely. The objective, therefore, is not to dock permanently in the security of one well-known port but to relax fearlessly into the ever-fluctuating waves and know that you float!

When we talk about feedback loops, repeating patterns, and spiralling experiences, I think it's worth noting that this is where many people lose hope in their meditation journeys. Being triggered by an incident, smell, or even an intrusive thought is commonplace if you have experienced some traumatic event. I often hear people say things like, "I thought I was over that," or "I thought I'd moved on," like somehow they haven't worked hard enough through their recovery to be *fixed* finally, or maybe they had hoped enough work would remove the scar from their heart. Scars are generally life-long. They may transform as the years pass until they are little more than a faded blemish, a suggestion of what once occurred, but they endure much like the grain and rings within a tree trunk. They tell the story of your life, growth, and fight to thrive. The reframing of our scars shows the distance travelled and how you react to the trigger each time matters. If you become increasingly enraged, disempowered, or hopeless each time you see it, you are likely (and almost certainly, inadvertently) generating the fuel or *"Sankhāra* (as termed in Buddhism)" for more fear-based responses in the future. We will explore this further in Chapter Seven, but for now, suffice it to say that passing repeatedly by the same triggers as you spiral upwards shouldn't surprise anyone. It's certainly no indication that you have taken a wrong turn. It's your opportunity, should you wish to take advantage of it, to test the distance travelled without expectation or judgement! It is also completely appropriate to decide "not yet." You don't need to engage with something to test yourself. You aren't required to force yourself through a healing process. If anything, that will only serve to prolong the healing process by stunting its efficacy.

Eventually though, if you observe that you have become less reactive to a trigger, that indicates that you are on the right path. Much like living with the grief of losing a loved one, it doesn't get easier with time; we become more compassionate with the experience of our grief because we know it only serves to demonstrate how deeply we've loved. So, with triggers, when we learn and train to be less reactive, we still observe their rise and fall. We still feel how they land in our bodies and psyches. They won't just disappear, but if we keep showing up and doing the work, one day, we'll come to a place where we'll experience them without the accompanying baggage of extreme emotional reaction, fear, physical contraction and other mental, social and spiritual impacts. We'll notice them come, notice them go and notice that we're still calm, relaxed and open despite their appearance and former control over us.

A word of caution on this: when discussing *Sankhāra*, it's important not to cultivate extreme positive or negative reactions. *Grasping* or *craving* is the opposite of *aversion*. The strong urge to turn away from something is the equal and opposite experience of figuratively running towards something, allowing desire to supersede sense. Of course, we should celebrate and enjoy things because life is for living. However, by observing rather than reacting, we make the equivalent of a carbon-neutral decision, with no negative trace or legacy. It's quite simply neutral. If this is how you'd like to experience your triggers in future or how you envisage feeling about your triggers once healed, then this is how to practise as a general approach, i.e. you must train your response of equanimity in all situations to access it in challenging situations.

Another note on healing: similar to triggers, most people have a skewed understanding and expectation of what healing is, should be, or will feel like. Healing comes when we learn to accept our experiences and truly embrace our true self in all its parts, without judgement or pre-conditions. Healing looks different for everyone, but most people conflate ideas of healing and invincibility against triggers as the same thing. While you can certainly reach that point through regular, sustained practice, this is somewhat elusive to the new practitioner and can lead to disappointment. 'Disappointment,' i.e. craving a different experience or outcome, is the cultivation of more 'Sankhāra.' If practising gratitude rewires our brain to look out for and notice more of what we are grateful for and realise what more we *can* be grateful for, then developing Sankhāra is the opposite practice of reacting mentally to all the things which we didn't like, seeing things that didn't turn out how we had hoped or even wanting more of something which is scarcity masquerading as pleasure. It's reinforcing the opposite of gratitude, cultivating a resentful 'me and my bad luck' mindset, entrenching a negative confirmation bias which becomes a super magnet attracting and perpetuating the experiences that we are simultaneously trying to move away from until pretty soon, it becomes all we can see and feel.

To ever experience true peace, rest, and healing, we must learn to reframe our expectations and experiences. We must understand the implications of our language and its power in shaping our actions through intentions. Using mantras, intention setting, and gratitude journalling are essential practices in training the brain away from fear and aversion and towards equanimity. We must peel back the layers of what we're saying and understand the conflict within our sentiments. For example, I once heard a straight-faced lady say, "I hate judgemental people."

Hate is a strong word that I deliberately choose not to use, but being able to identify the subtle irony of someone consciously judging that others are worthy of receiving hate because they have deemed them to be too judgmental was one of the first times I realised how completely egocentric we are as a species; and that we are often completely unaware of how the things we dislike in other people are subconsciously the things we dislike about ourselves.

What we may not realise when we cultivate these judgements about other people is that we are simultaneously narrowing the parameters of our own behaviour that we find acceptable to fit in and feel safe. We need to be cautious about sanitising our identity in this way. It doesn't take much before we find ourselves lost and completely without any reference points as to *who we are*.

Chapter Three

What's Love Got To Do With It?

I mentioned earlier that I was in a stilt-walking samba band (created by circus performers who could all walk on stilts - an impressive sight!). After taking adult circus classes at the Belfast Community Circus School, I joined this band. Nura, the band leader at the time, was also a teacher at the circus school, and I wasn't invited to practise as much as I was asked to make up the numbers for a gig. I had been given a pair of *Dura Stilts* for Christmas. Dura stilts are rectangular-framed metal stilts with buckles, hinges and broad, flat feet. They're much easier to walk on than the traditional wooden peg circus stilts, especially if you're an absolute beginner. However, they are also much heavier, so they're not ideal when walking for miles carrying drums. I'd heard some plasterers and tradespeople use them on building sites, and I thought, "Hey, they can't be that difficult to learn."

Truth be told, I'd never used them before I was asked to do the gig. I had just two weeks to learn how to walk on these beasts before my debut performance, so I got to work. Fast forward to the gig; it was an Easter Spring Fling in Bangor, a seaside town on the northeast coast of County Down in Northern Ireland. The weather was stormy, windy and wet, and I knew I was in for a baptism of fire, albeit a very soggy one!

When I arrived to meet the band, I could hear rolls of parcel tape being stretched and wrapped as the stilt walkers attached the stilts to their feet and legs. Over the next few years, I became very familiar with that sound and grew fond of it because of its association with this pastime.

Through this group, I met my first authentic tribe, people I knew and chose to spend time with. I developed valuable relationships in the circus and samba community that would revolutionise my understanding, expectations of, and approach to platonic intimacy. Of course, I didn't know that at the time. All I knew was how much I adored these people, and the more I got to know them, the deeper my sense of connection and love for them grew.

One of these remarkable individuals, a Surdo (massive bass drum) player from County Westmeath in the South of Ireland, was called Aoife. She is almost puppy-like in demeanour in that she's excitable, affectionate and fun to be around - even more so when she grows into her big dog paws! We were hanging out after a samba gig one afternoon, enjoying a pint with a few other samba-heads, when Aoife mentioned planning to take part in the Mongol Rally, a once-in-a-lifetime, 10,000-mile trip in a one-litre vehicle. As she outlined the plan, I asked to hear more about it and became increasingly enchanted with the idea.

"Sounds amazing," I said, almost reticently. "I would love to do something like that."

Aoife didn't skip a beat. "Why don't you?"

As I said before, I practised taking my time to hear a question, listening for a moment to hear my genuine answer and aiming to articulate myself as precisely as possible. After a few moments' pause, I realised I had drawn a complete blank. As I put it, I didn't have a reasonable excuse not to "do something like that." It took me thirty minutes to drive home after that chat, and by the time I got back to my then-partner (now husband, "Skinner"), I had made up my mind. I was going to take part in the Mongol Rally. I didn't know how I would raise the money I needed if Aoife had invited me to join her team, or if I would have to start from scratch in finding my own team, but it didn't matter. My mind was made up.

I wasn't sure what reaction I would get from Skinner, but I knew we had to have the conversation. We lived together and had already been through a lot as a couple. We had been partners for seven years, and, no doubt, that "seven-year itch" mindset crept into his thoughts at some point as I outlined my ambitions. But, gracious as ever, he set aside his concerns and focused on how best to support me.

I realised through our conversation how our different social backgrounds shaped our individual perspectives on the subject. I felt it was a huge undertaking and not for "someone like me." I assumed it would be a mammoth struggle to raise thousands of pounds for such a trip. Having already trekked across the Sahara (among other travel-based adventures), Skinner knew this was nonsense. It was he who talked me into doing a skydive with him and his friends. At the time, I had assumed that this, too, was out of reach for "someone like me."

So, my advice is, if you're ever in a position where you'd like to do something that seems unrealistic, speak with someone who is doing it or has already done it. It's not unusual for things which are beyond your frame of reference to seem like they're entirely unattainable. I'm a big fan of this perspective; it's part of the reason I loved training in the circus, learning the art of the impossible. Remember:

"People who say it cannot be done, should not interrupt those who are doing it." George Bernard Shaw

In working-class communities, people often find it difficult to progress beyond cycles of poverty due to a lack of 'linking capital,' i.e. social infrastructure. This can mean various things, but most often, it's the lack of access to meaningful relationships with people in a position of authority or privilege. It's like they're outside a locked door and, having never been through it, they can't even imagine what might be on the other side. This hinders their capacity to reach their fullest potential. Skinner and I discussed how I might make this trip happen, and by the end of the conversation, I knew I had his full support. I was going to do this!

Truthfully, my husband has always been my biggest supporter and champion, beyond my parents. Reflecting on our almost twenty years together, I can see how we have weaved this relationship as a safety net for each other to reach dizzying new heights continually. When people say things like "my better half" and "he makes me feel whole," I wince and cringe. I've never liked the idea of relying on anyone other than myself and am equally averse to anyone relying on me like I'm the air they breathe or they couldn't cope without me. I've since learned that this degree of hyper-independence is, in fact, a trauma response.

However, in my relationship with my husband, I can at least understand where that dependency language comes from. I would express it differently, though. Skinner and I don't agree on anything other than how to treat people. We are polar opposites regarding our interests, beliefs and outlooks. Still, we are crystal clear on our individual values, which are in complete and absolute alignment. This, matched with the unconditional love we have committed to each other through our wedding vows and even before then, is the foundation for our happiness and successes.

I spoke with Aoife and told her I would love to join her Rally team. She promptly introduced me to our third team member and fellow samba-head, Elaine. We spent the next nine months organising fundraisers, raising our profile, seeking sponsorship for a vehicle and supplies, completing visa paperwork and, of course, getting many travel vaccinations. Before we knew it, we were setting off on the trip of a lifetime. I kept a journal, and I'll publish the whole story someday. It's the book I was supposed to be writing when this one emerged, but some relevant, key learnings from the trip tie in nicely with this story, so I'll speak to those briefly before we move on. To learn more about that trip, search "Taillte Tank Girls" on Facebook for our profile and some photos.

Chapter Four

The Road Less Travelled

One of the first things we noticed when we arrived at the launch party for the Mongol Rally 2013 and the start line of Bodrum Castle in the South of England was that we, as women, were significantly outnumbered by easily 50:1. We were an all-female team of three. We could count on one hand how many teams were like us. More often, there would be teams that included one female.

It wasn't until we were at the European "Czech out party" in the Czech Republic, having a chat over beers in the wee small hours of the morning, that we articulated this. We talked about how each of us was in a relationship with a guy back home and how this "sausage fest," as one of the girls called it, was going to be a long couple of months of turning down sexual advances, offers and invitations. Before we left, it hadn't occurred to me that this trip would be so heavily gendered. I hadn't considered that I would need to decline advances constantly, and sure enough, it felt like almost every fella that we didn't connect meaningfully with did "chance their arm," throwing out the odd chat-up line or moving in closer after a few drinks, just in case they might strike lucky. I say every fella we didn't connect with because those we formed mutual connections with became good friends, allies, brothers and kin as if we'd known each other our entire lives.

This experience helped me broaden my understanding of platonic intimacy and the need for loving relationships beyond family, romantic and sexual contexts. Sharing love with others is integral to the human experience, but I have generally only found this sentiment expressed through religious texts and discourse. Exploring the concept with my fellow adventurers, I realised that the cultural discourse around it, as I had understood it, was utterly skewed. I now call it "The con of monogamy." Typically, when I say this, people jump to the assumption that I am polyamorous, but that's not accurate, and it's not how I would term it. Let me explain.

I had learned over my lifetime (I was twenty-nine at the time) that you spend your life looking for your "one true love." When you find them, no one else will compare, and you never want to be apart. A real fairytale perspective, wouldn't you agree? I recognised these feelings during the first few years of dating Skinner and in previous relationships. In that exciting stage, you're consumed with thoughts of each other and giddy when contact is made. I've heard it described as "sticky love," which feels apt.

In looking for that deep, authentic connection with another, many of us, over time, begin to de-prioritise our friendships and hobbies, making less time for others outside of our romantic unit so that we can fall stupidly in love! And then what? Perhaps that relationship runs its course or comes to a natural conclusion. Then we realise we're left with zero social connections or places where we feel like we fit in. Or, we end up creating a family unit with that person and give more and more of ourselves over because we don't even know who we are anymore. We assume that's what everyone else is doing. I say this because I've seen it repeatedly and experienced much of it myself.

However, when I started attending circus school and samba practice, I would come home and tell Skinner, "Aww, this guy or that girl...I love them so much!" I understood that coming home and saying such a thing out of context could be challenging and potentially hurtful to hear. I also knew how important it was to tell the truth and acknowledge these feelings of connection and intimacy to myself and my husband because hiding them might create a rift between us. That was a gamble I wasn't prepared to take.

Thankfully, Skinner, being the man he is, accompanied me to my circus and samba gigs for the first few years, entirely at my request. This may sound more like controlling than supporting, so I want to be clear: I was terrified of doing these gigs as much for the danger aspect as for the fact of being visible. I always asked him to come with me. His confidence in me was tangible and contagious. I had developed severe aversions to performing or being visible generally over the years. If I hadn't had his encouragement, faith and companionship, these are roads which I likely would never have ventured down. Fear would've won, and I'd have lost many opportunities for growth and self-acceptance.

By attending these events with me, Skinner got to know the characters I had described and, over time, he articulated similar feelings. We'd come home from gigs and dote on the people we'd spent our day with. Looking back now, I can see how we were developing a culture around platonic intimacy within our relationship that I rarely see expressed in mainstream constructs, but at the time, we were feeling into who and how we were. We both recognised that 'circus' was a far cry from where we had grown up and when we found ourselves there, we knew it felt right. We realised we were in the middle of a pretty special community and, perhaps more subtly, a life-altering transition.

The moment I knew this wasn't solely a phenomenon based on the people I liked and whom Skinner had learned to like was when he came home from work and told me about one of his colleagues. "She's brilliant," he said. "I love her!" I remember feeling proud to be trusted with such honesty, thrilled that my husband could find a joyful connection with another, and excited to believe that we could continue to develop authentic, deep connections with people beyond the construct we first recognised it in. The potential was tangible and infinite, and that was very exciting!

I had never experienced this in my previous relationships and had felt my fair share of jealousy, suspicion and fear from such situations. But when I think of it, that was all during my teenage years. Through my mindfulness meditation practice, I knew I didn't have to engage with these feelings as they were nothing more than fleeting distractions, so I intentionally chose not to cultivate that energy. Funnily enough, someone recently accused me of creating "drama" (it was meant to be a derogatory slight), and I thought, "Man, it's been almost twenty years since I've even heard that word, let alone been accused of being responsible for it. Nice try, but you are definitely barking up the wrong tree there!"

For the sake of being explicit, if you're new to meditation, it's worth pointing out that you can have up to 10,000 negative thoughts each day. They are constantly running in the back of your mind; you won't hear them all, but they vastly outnumber the positive thoughts. The point is, these thoughts are generally useless; they aren't fact or necessarily what you believe. They just come up. If you are in a reactionary state, you maybe haven't been eating or sleeping well, or you're upset over something completely unrelated; these thoughts will keep surfacing. What can often happen is that we attach feelings from something else to these irrelevant thoughts that arise. Before you know it, we're reacting to something meaningless in an altogether irrational and disproportionate way.

Our previous encounters inform our nervous system about how safe any new experience is likely to be, and we're constantly scanning our environment and interactions for safety cues on the subconscious level. How reactive we are to any given situation is directly linked to the state of our nervous system, which is ever-changing, depending on the circumstance and company we find ourselves in.

If we are in a *Dorsal Vagal* state (also known as sympathetic nervous system activation), we can and will perceive anything as a threat. That means our nervous system is already cued up for a fight or flight response to incoming stimuli, and our ability to accurately interpret other people's social cues (or social engagement systems, a term coined by the father of *Polyvagal Theory, Stephen Porges)* is negatively impacted.

Conversely, if we are in a *Ventral Vagal* state (also referred to as parasympathetic nervous system activation), our nervous system has assessed the situation as safe; we are in rest and digest mode, where we can access states of play, collaboration, connection and, importantly, change.

So, upon hearing Skinner say these words about loving someone other than me and noticing that my default reaction to it was one of excitement for him - of warmth, relief, and hope - is a moment that I will remember for the rest of my life. Recognising later that I had migrated from the dysregulated state of a teenager to a self and co-regulated state in this relationship with my partner when I could just as easily have interpreted the stimulus as a threat or challenge due to past experiences, was notable only by the fact that this was an entirely novel and conflict-free experience.

Some of you may have read that last piece and perhaps crumpled a little where you sit; maybe you held your breath and braced yourself for the worst. I invite you to quickly check in with yourself and see how you feel after reading this far.

What do you feel in your body, and where? If you are reading this book, I'll assume that you are interested in these practices and have some basic knowledge, but for those who have picked up this book and are completely new to mindfulness practices, the following advice may help.

* * *

If you're ready to begin a short practice, it's a good idea to start by noticing where on your body you can feel and also notice where you can't feel. After making a mental note of this, you can either re-adjust your posture to a comfortable upright position, seated or standing or, if you're familiar with such a concept, use the breath to reinflate your structure.

Once settled, feel your sit bones on the chair or your feet on the floor. Turn your eyes downwards or close them completely if that feels safe for you today. Bring your attention to your breath.

Firstly, notice the quality of your breath. How would you describe it? Is it smooth or ragged, shallow or deep, forceful or gentle?

Next, allow your attention to rest on your abdomen, between the bottom of your ribcage and the top of your pelvis.

As you continue to breathe (ideally, in through the nose and out through a relaxed, slightly open mouth), follow the inhale all the way down to the tummy. On the exhale, aim to sigh a sense of relief without making the exhale a muscle action.

If your mind wanders, as it inevitably will, gently and patiently pull your attention back to your breath.

With practice and focus on the breath, thoughts eventually slow down. The less you engage with these thoughts, the more stillness and calmness you can access and the deeper your relaxation. Generally, your intuitive thoughts will arise from the tranquillity of this highly open and creative state.

After a few moments of this practice, you may notice what part of your body is distracting you. In this stillness, you may realise why there is an ache or dullness; for example, you might remember mindlessly bumping into a wall or getting up awkwardly from a chair. With enough practice, you can come to a place of quiet and stillness on command and discover what needs tending to. Sometimes, the answers come hours, days and weeks later, or you might wait years to understand one strand of enquiry fully. So, cultivating patience and turning up without any preconceived agenda or goal is an important and fundamental aspect of this practice.

* * *

Of course, you can meditate with and on intentions, too, but that is a different practice from the one I am describing here.

So, if you have been able to observe how this book has landed in your body so far and the complex range of reactions you've had to the content, framed by your filters of experiences, biases, and resourcefulness, then you can use all of that data to learn more about yourself. It is through this work that we begin to identify who we are in auto-pilot and piece together the patterns of how we react out of deep-seated fear, trauma, and societal and familial conditioning.

This painstaking job of untangling ourselves from the ego, the expectations of others, and the fear of who we have the potential to become is not for the faint-hearted. But it will pay off tenfold if we stick with it, learning how to replace and create more healthy, proportionate and relevant behaviours in response to challenging scenarios and habitual thought patterns. How much would you love to be able to decide and design the way you react in times of stress, uncertainty and fear?

In considering the relationship content we've just explored, sometimes people are surprised to identify sensations of collapse, rigidity, or a rabbit-in-the-headlights kind of stuckness. Indeed, we all oscillate between nervous system regulation and dysregulation throughout the day in micro-episodes, so please don't be alarmed to uncover such a reaction. These micro-episodes are easily observable when scrolling through social media, for example. You don't get a say in all the content that appears on your feed, and there have been occasions when I've inadvertently caught sight of something that really should've had a trigger warning or some mechanism for allowing me to choose if I consented to consuming that content.

Notice the physiological changes in your body as you scroll on social media. Do you accidentally hold your breath? Do the muscles around your ribcage clench a little? Do your shoulders rise automatically to protect your neck and throat like you're in imminent danger? We want to learn to identify these indicators to the relentless, incoming stimuli and implement strategies to self-regulate at the earliest opportunity to remain at the helm of our own ship.

The reactions described above are standard responses to affection and intimacy, especially if you have experienced a relationship breakdown or a safety violation. Pay close attention to how the words and sensations around relationships arise in your body because they can inform you about what you subconsciously communicate to other people's nervous systems. By embodying an exaggeration of this *collapse* posture of defeat, insecurity, resentment, and even hostility, some of us actively sabotage any chance of welcoming love into our lives.

Been there, done that!

A clarification about meditation practice: Many people say, “I can’t meditate,” and of course, they mean, “I can’t quiet my mind on demand,” which is not the same thing. In all seriousness, if you’ve only tried meditation a handful of times, it’s also a wildly unreasonable expectation. Monks don’t live in monasteries, dedicating years to learning a practice that any random punter could pick up and master in a four-week course.

The practice of turning up to meditate *is* meditating. Thoughts arising is an essential component of the practice. You would be unable to practise if thoughts didn’t arrive. They are, in fact, the fuel for your practice, and when they finally subside, which they inevitably will if you continue to turn up, they will also be the measure of your practice. You will notice more readily when the mind becomes noisy again and know you have the tools to manage that. And here comes some of that delightfully confusing contradiction I mentioned at the start!

Busy thoughts don't necessarily mean you're not successful in your practice either, so don't allow yourself to be derailed by surprise instances of disquiet. Predictably, your "monkey mind" in meditation will try to distract, defeat, or redirect you to other, more pressing (yet exceedingly trivial) matters. If anything, this indicates that you're close to breaking the shackles of ego, and the ego doesn't want to lose its position at the top of your hierarchy. I revisit this idea and discourse of monkey-mind distraction tactics in Chapter Seven.

As with anything in mindfulness-based meditation, it's not the stimulant you need to focus on; it's your reaction to it. Many people who try meditating veer off track when they begin to pursue the Bliss sensation of Stage Two, instead of committing to the most important task of the practice – consistently turning up without judgement and preconditions – which is the sole task of the practice at every stage.

A note about ego: Throughout this book, you will encounter references to the ego and its tendency to take control and dictate decisions. The ego itself isn't inherently bad; rather, it simply needs to be kept in balance.

Chapter Five

Learning to Read the Nervous System

What follows is a very personal example of how I observed the dorsal vagal shutdown and collapse response around intimacy in myself.

I had noticed how comfortable my circus and samba friends were in physical proximity to one another. Hugs, a two-armed, full-frontal embrace, were a central feature of this group's communication, and I used to become rigid in response to them. I didn't want hugs, but I didn't want to hurt anyone's feelings either. It wasn't personal; I just didn't want any physical intimacy from these people I adored and admired. What a weird thing for a human to say!

This was another trauma pattern surfacing, and in coming to that realisation, I committed to unlearning it or, rather, deliberately exploring healthier replacement patterns. Some might say that I've since gone full-tilt to the opposite side of the scale as I now embrace anyone or anything that will allow me, but it took a concerted effort and dedicated practice to show up and face this hurt continually; to choose to drop my barriers and explore the unknown with non-judgement and self-compassion. The challenge and the practice were observing what arose for me in these hugs that I had been unaware of. What feelings were bubbling up just below the surface? Why was my nervous system saying, "Hell no!"?

Typically, when you find yourself in an environment or circumstance that has historically proven dangerous and bad for you, it is common to freeze, disassociate and mentally retreat until the danger has passed. This is a safety override function of the autonomic (or automatic) nervous system, which means that it's a process we can't deliberately direct, though we can influence what additional data the nervous system receives to make a more balanced interpretation, using breathwork, embodiment & mindfulness; stacking the deck if you will, to mitigate cues of non-safety and regulate your nervous system in real-time. Pursuing these practices is important, even when you feel you no longer need them, so your tank is full when you need to deploy them.

If you're interested in this topic, I highly recommend looking into *Stephen Porge's "Polyvagal Theory."*

Learning to be present in giving and receiving a hug required me to override my body's instincts to shelter me from intrusion. It required me to un-numb and feel what was occurring. It didn't happen overnight, of course, but it did happen. When my friends caught wind of this, they queued up in the juggling hall to hug me, knowing it would be the sincerest, most heartfelt hug I could muster.

One quick distinction on this for accuracy: when I say I hugged people despite the feedback I was getting from my body, that's neither entirely accurate nor entirely untrue; it's somewhere in between. Often, what can happen is we get stuck in a cycle of dorsal vagal activation where the nervous system is applying these extreme measures, tactics and filters for protection long after the danger (or perceived danger) has passed and beyond when the perspective has outrun its efficacy. So it was never a case of me bull-headedly ignoring the sensory feedback I was observing; it was always with a measure of "have I outgrown this perspective? How real are the threats that my body is telling me it perceives?"

I always advocate listening to your body and taking your cues from there but recognise that you can misinterpret the cues, so don't be afraid to change tack. There is no shame in upgrading your perspective to a more mature understanding. Isn't that the beauty of getting older and learning - both luxuries are guaranteed to no one?

Back to the rally: we made friends with several really class lads and a handful of other women. There were two guys that I felt connected to. I adored them. I made sure they were aware from the outset that there was zero chance of anything sexual or romantic happening between us. I'm a pretty pragmatic person, and I'm happy to blurt out awkward truths which, as mentioned before, is an oversharing symptom of ADHD. Nonetheless, I intentionally defined my boundaries, outlined my terms of engagement and managed expectations. I wouldn't have tried to be so transparent if I hadn't liked them. These guys may or may not have believed me and may or may not have even been interested in anything other than my company, but they respected what I said, and we decidedly made the most of our time together when our paths crossed. We didn't always travel together, but at random points along the route across a third of the earth's circumference, we shared some beautiful moments as our stories and paths intertwined: breathtaking sunsets, challenging terrains, small victories, cuddles, kindness and admiration.

This was the three-month trip of a lifetime, and I wholly expected it to alter my perspective. There were so many instances where I had to dig deep to regulate myself and support my teammates. Other times, I was the reason we were all so dysregulated. We were, occasionally, a little out of our depth. Yet, we all somehow made it to Ulaanbaatar, the capital city of Mongolia, in our Nissan Micra, which we named "Fawlty." Along the route, we were frequently reminded of the many teams that had faltered long before us as we stumbled across abandoned rally vehicles with team members' names scratched out or taped over. We knew we were lucky to get as far as we did, and we didn't take anything for granted!

One example where I remember needing to have a serious word with myself was when we were in the eastern region of Turkey, around Cappadocia. We were trying to have breakfast, "filling our boots" for the day's adventuring, when we were suddenly plagued by wasps. It felt like hundreds of these tiny, ferocious little gremlins came deliberately to have breakfast with us or, more accurately, have breakfast from us. You'd have thought we were intruding on them the way they took over the place. Perhaps that's exactly how they saw it. And the Turks know how to do breakfast! There was an alfresco buffet with everything you could want: fresh fruits, olives, cheeses, jams, meats, eggs, juices, coffee, and fresh bread with seeds. I was so looking forward to it. I sat at the table, and within minutes, I had reached my limit. I was so stressed, anxious and fearful of these wasps. They were diving at my face and crawling on my friend's jam toast as she moved it towards her open mouth; they were everywhere, and I was not coping!

My two teammates didn't bat an eyelid at our uninvited guests and encouraged me to relax and enjoy breakfast. I said I would be back shortly and excused myself from the table. Having found a quiet spot in the shade, away from the food and the swarm of winged thieves, I sat down to quietly meditate. I'm not sure what I was hoping would happen or why I even chose to do it, but after some fifteen minutes on my own, observing my breath, noticing when my thoughts were reactions to stimulants, and intentionally restoring integrity to my posture, I was able to return to the breakfast table, to the exact same set of circumstances and I felt completely different. I was calm. I felt anchored and was much less easily frustrated or rattled. I could sit for the next twenty minutes and enjoy my breakfast. I surprised myself.

By the time we had finished eating and set off on our day, I felt like I had turned a corner in my practice. It was no longer a practice of skills acquisition; I was now in the early stages of integrating what I knew and tailoring it to my needs. It was intuitive to remove myself from the situation and resource myself by drawing from that well. I now know this is often taught as the best way to self-regulate, especially if you are raising children and find yourself struggling with or triggered by their behaviour. Yet this often isn't taught culturally, and instead, we're led to believe that we must stay in contentious situations, allowing ourselves to be triggered, often re-traumatising ourselves and others to save face, to maintain a degree of civility and to meet the expectations of others. Ironically, this is sometimes described as “keeping the peace!”

This experience taught me how that approach is a false economy, and where possible, the priority is to self-regulate, even if you have to remove yourself briefly from the company to do so because the difference between my before and after in this instance showed me very clearly how the exact same event can be perceived differently by the same person depending on how you’re framing it, and the multiple degrees of varying tension(s) you’re bringing to the event at any given moment.

If you can learn to cultivate your internal environment to filter stress out as it occurs in the body and convert it before it has a chance to settle in and trust me, I’m still learning to apply this myself, you will experience much less resistance, friction and stress in your daily life. I have seen this proven repeatedly since first observing it in my own life.

One of my other notable traits, which I had the opportunity to explore on this trip of a lifetime, was the idea of having control. Through my meditation practice over the last year, I noticed how tightly I was clinging to the idea of having control in all instances and circumstances. I recognised this habit from my parental home and, with the environment my parents were working to raise a young family in, who could blame them? It served a purpose for a time; raising five small children through the 1970s to the 1990s in Northern

Ireland was nothing if not challenging. There was so much to balance, juggle and manage, but the idea of being in or having control is often nothing more than an illusion, a security blanket we wrap around a very narrow context so that we can tell ourselves that we're covered.

I began to regard the idea of having control as unsustainable, counterproductive and inherently flawed, so to acknowledge that I had a default bias towards this type of perspective or delusion was pretty cutting. It wasn't an attribute that I was keen to continue cultivating, but I was glad to recognise it and know that I didn't have to subject myself to a life of unnecessary friction and turmoil; to know that I could find space and soften the edges that were undoubtedly doing more to fence me in than keep any real danger out. Some people refer to this experience as a state of surrender, and this is a concept we will return to throughout the rest of the book.

I made a conscious decision to approach this road trip to flip the script. On the road, there would be no control. Before we set off, we roughly estimated the route to apply for our visas. We made a list of essential kit, and managed to get everything we needed from sponsors. After that, I concluded that there would be very little else I could influence, let alone control, along the way.

Having been a strict vegetarian for some eighteen years before this trip, and having read some blogs from previous teams who'd taken part in the Mongol Rally, I became aware that I may not have the freedom and choice over my food consumption that I typically enjoy at home and I really leaned into my discomfort on this. I resolved to take each meal as it came and to do my best. What would be, would be. This outlook set the bar for my tolerance to other variables; if I could forgo one of my core values for these three months, I could see where else there might be room for stretch, new learning and growth.

Mostly, I didn't have much of an issue with food since we camped wild and shopped at the local markets we drove past almost daily. We generally ate very well, dining on fresh, seasonal produce and juicy, ripe melon. Apart from occasions when we were invited to dine in with the locals or passed through big cities where we couldn't set up our camp gear to cook, we were entirely self-sufficient for food. Whenever we met other rally teams and invited them to join us for dinner, they were super impressed and surprised by our one-pot meals and al fresco dining setup. One team that we ate with in the middle of the Karakum desert in Turkmenistan couldn't quite believe that we were setting up to cook a fresh, vegan, gluten-free, hot meal for ten people on our authentic Persian rug in the middle of the desert, in pitch darkness with a single gas hob when so far, they had only used their camp stoves for boiling water to rehydrate noodles!

However, I recall one time in Mongolia when I ordered a plate of potato salad as it was the only vegetarian option on the menu. The salad was laced with what I call "surprise mutton," and it was overpoweringly aromatic to my meat-starved senses. As soon as I clocked it, I handed the dish over to one of the girls, and it was quickly devoured.

Something I learned on this trip about my relationship with food was that I used to think I would get "hangry" if I didn't have a satisfactory meal or snack approximately every four hours. Well, that belief was well and truly decimated by the time I got home. I soon realised that, between growing up with the transgenerational trauma of famine in my country, along with now being a vegetarian from a deeply agricultural homeland, I had developed a scarcity mentality around food, which I wasn't aware of until I met my husband, Skinner. He didn't have the same relationship with food as I did, which I had never recognised in such sharp relief before.

Relinquishing all control over food was a massive step for me, but what I learned about myself in the process would someday contribute to an ability to drop into a flow state of surrender and tranquillity at any given point, despite what else might be going on environmentally.

We never know definitively how things will turn out until they come to pass, and yet, many of us spend our time white-knuckling against it, trying to control, protect and defend ourselves and the things we love from anything that could threaten or seek to cause harm. I believe this ambition and outlook are numbing and destructive, even under the guise of preservation. It can stop us from trying new things, exploring aspects of our identity and evolving into the versions of ourselves that we've been too fearful to even dream of. When we learn to embrace our intuition and practice being okay with wholeheartedly investing ourselves into something, even when we can't explain it, we learn how to access a state of surrender, acceptance and detachment in a very authentic and seamless way. This feeling arises in the bliss stage, Stage Two of spiritual awakening, and links back to Stage Five, *Groundedness*, but we're not quite there yet.

When I returned home from the Mongol Rally, suffice it to say, things in my life looked very different. By that, I mean I couldn't regard anything through the lenses I'd previously used. My life appeared not to have changed from the outside initially, and yet I knew that nothing would be the same again. I spent weeks, if not months, in a hibernation phase, which at the time I had put down to the culture shock of returning to Western society after months of becoming less and less "civilised." I use inverted commas here because I've come to regard Western culture as rampant, excessive, and, for the most part, quite toxic. We have become so far removed from much of the natural function and process of human existence in pursuit of perceived comfort, predictability, and hoarding of natural resources that it is now inarguably having an enormously detrimental impact on our health, our planet and the future integrity of the human race. It feels like such a perversion of how we are meant to live that it sometimes leaves me dizzy. So, to say I struggled to get back into "normal life" after the Mongol Rally would be a massive understatement. Sure enough, I emerged gradually from this place of overwhelm to start living the changes I had accumulated and catalysed throughout the trip.

This stage in the journey can be described as Stage Four of Meditation, which is called "*The Void*" or emptiness; when you feel completely adrift and cut off from your practices. However, because I was exhausted from my trip and, at the same time, so glad to be home, I didn't fight this stage or worry about why I felt the way I did. Instead, I succumbed to the rest and minimal sensory stimulation I needed. And it's funny because sometimes these stages of awakening don't follow a logical sequence. In this case, it felt like my mind and consciousness were playing catch up to the wisdom I had tuned into within my body. Even more interestingly, perhaps, I have observed over the proceeding years how these cycles can sometimes run concurrently, depending on your practices, appetite for active self-healing and post-traumatic growth. So at times, I have been able to notice when I am in a *Bliss* stage from learning a new practice, for example, training in a new martial art or learning flow-based circus arts, whilst also moving beyond *Groundedness* (Stage Five), into *Purpose and Mission* (Stage Six) from a previous cycle, for example, training in Yoga Therapy, working with marginalised youth or writing this book.

It can feel a bit disorientating when you don't know that these things happen, not necessarily in logical order, and there may be concurrent, overlapping processes operating at different stages during the same period. Again, to fixate on ideas of "I thought I was past this" or "I've done so much work, I shouldn't be back here" only serves as a temporary distraction and causes unnecessary suffering, which you'll hear referred to as *Duḥkha* in Buddhist traditions.

After my return home, I took on various professional roles, and my career progressed in line with my ambition to alleviate Duḥkha or suffering wherever possible, supporting the most vulnerable. Some of the lessons of this once-in-a-lifetime trip were still quietly percolating in the background. Like a river that has etched its way through dense rock over centuries, this new knowing was slowly forging freshly carved gorges of wisdom in my soul. When the opportunity arose in 2014 to sign up for a Yoga Teacher Training Course with my favourite yoga teacher, I couldn't wait to get involved.

I had always thought of doing teacher training as a hobby or semi-retirement plan for a time way off in the future. So, when the prospectus came through, I was thrilled to think I could get a head start on that. Little did I know that this would be a huge turning point in my personal, professional and spiritual development. I spent four years and four hundred hours studying yoga, progressing on to yoga therapy. We trained for one full weekend per month, and during this time, as I climbed the career ladder in the community voluntary sector, I came to rely heavily on my training weekends to recharge and reset my body and mind for the invariable incoming challenges of my many public-facing roles.

I noticed that the more complex my job became, the more resilient I had the luxury of being, resourced by my commitment to my own well-being and practices. Due to such significant shifts in my perspectives, I found contentious conversations almost amusing. I was able to listen objectively, hear highly emotive information without taking it personally, rationalise a way forward by sensitively understanding conflicting agendas, and mediate some hot and heavy stand-offs. This became my new baseline, and I credited all of this newfound patience and pragmatism to my meditation practice. Ironically, when I didn't feel so well-resourced, I also blamed that on my meditation practice, but maybe not in the way you would think.

I spent years working in roles that required me to advocate for the rights and needs of others. Most often, I did that for 'the other'" community from which I would be recognised in that post-conflict setting. I inherently believed that this choice was the only way to ensure that we could continue developing towards a peaceful and mutually beneficial future. In Northern Ireland, we call this "cross-community work." However, this brought a more nuanced and less obvious set of complications. For one, those who regarded themselves as having the same community background as me, often saw my work as an outright and absolute betrayal, not to mention entirely and unnecessarily dangerous. Conversely, those I worked for and with typically regarded my efforts with cynicism, distrust, and a deep-seated contempt, which they were rarely ever in a position to recognise personally, let alone acknowledge to me; it was so engrained in their outlook.

I spent a lot of time fencing myself off from these mistruths, trusting that the work I was doing was good enough to speak for itself, without explanation. This kind of self-resourcing took a lot of commitment on my part, which was why I was so grateful for the dedicated monthly resets of yoga teacher training weekends. When my training finished, I became increasingly unclear of the reasons why this should be the ambition; why my efforts were continually misconstrued and distorted to suit a narrative that was entirely unfamiliar to me, and perhaps most hurtfully, by the people I was there to support. Gradually, I began to regard my meditation practice as something which was facilitating other people's abuse of my patience and tolerance. Or was it that my practice was enabling them to conduct themselves without consciousness or consequence? I felt that my deeper experience of meditation practice was creating the conditions for people to trample over the top of me without a second thought about how destructive that was.

My body ached for fairness, and the more I craved it, the less available it seemed. So, I stopped meditating. I knew I would have to redefine my terms of engagement in line with what I now found acceptable, that a good and robust practice shouldn't leave me feeling so depleted and disposable. This was another massive shift for me that I wholeheartedly undertook after yet another Stage Three episode of "Dark Night of the Soul."

It's worth relating this experience to what I had described earlier about safety cues and outworkings of the autonomic nervous system. I can recognise now, as I look back, that I had moved from a highly regulated state fuelled by monthly weekend resets, to a chronically dysregulated state when I didn't have the dedicated, regular practice and, perhaps more importantly when I didn't have my teacher to call on for clarity or to co-regulate with. My state of dysregulation was impacting my ability to perceive my environment as safe, and at the same time, my literally and genuinely unsafe environment was making it difficult for me to regulate my nervous system as I had previously been doing.

It would've been unwise to continue pushing myself into a practice that I felt was leading me to dysregulation when I knew it didn't feel safe. That's one of the most important aspects of sharing these stories with you, so that you will learn not to doubt yourself when you need to change things up and make counterintuitive adjustments where needed.

"Until you make the unconscious conscious, it will direct your life and you will call it fate." Carl Jung

---

It's episodes like this, where I have waded through experiences of my practice, being more triggered than regulated, and trusting myself to know that I shouldn't continue to force myself through an experience which everyone says will be good for me, that I have come to term myself as a 'trauma-informed' practitioner. I have spent decades working at the grassroots community level across Northern Ireland. I know what trauma looks like, sounds like and feels like. Through my studies, be that in yoga, meditation, sound therapy, polyvagal theory or martial arts, I've learned to identify and recognise the states and stages that I've been through, and I have a range of vocabulary I can draw on to describe the same experiences as I identify them in others. Only when we know these episodes intimately and understand the variations of how they manifest are we able to assist others safely through that process.

Before moving on, it's important to emphasise co-regulating with your teacher or guide. It's so very subtle in the initial stages that it's barely identifiable but something I have come to understand is that there are many reasons to have the support of a teacher; to have someone you can ask questions of, share your doubts with and fast track your learning so that you don't fall foul to monkey-mind distraction techniques or take a wrong turn. The list is endless, but for me, one of the most essential things about finding a good teacher, the right teacher for you, is to find a frequency that matches what you're aiming to cultivate. In doing this, it means that even if you find yourself in a situation as I've just described, where you're practice isn't robust enough to counteract the energy coming at you, you can still reset simply by being in the company of your teacher. Your nervous system will entrain to theirs. You will be able to access healing and safe states more readily, and you'll be able to navigate the dense territory of doubt with hope, reassurance and support. More than that, you can cultivate a familiarity with what those states *feel* like, which is critical to creating pathways that will enable you to return to those states unaided... eventually.

Much of what I have learned, I have done so alone, and I believe that much of it is a personal and solo journey; you have to put in the hours if you are going to truly understand and believe the truth of what you uncover, but good teachers are worth their weight in gold if for nothing more than their transmittable, dedicated and curated frequencies, which are a key reference point and baseline when everything else inevitably upends.

Chapter Six

Making It Relevant

When I started my Yoga Teacher Training, I already knew one of the three teachers on the course, Lisa. I had no idea at the time how lucky I was to study under one of the other instructors, Marie Quail, who began training Yoga Teachers in Northern Ireland in 1995. The Good Friday Peace Agreement didn't come about until 1998, so Belfast was a far cry from an Indian Ashram or Buddhist Temple.

Marie is the embodiment of soft strength. She's almost feline in her movement and has an understated glamour, coupled with the unmistakable glow of someone who enjoys life's luxuries but isn't using them as distractions or facades. She has done the work and is very well respected, locally and internationally. I felt so honoured to train with her in person after our first lesson, and that was before I knew what an incredibly talented teacher and mentor she was. The way she holds space and guides you to your own revelations was something that I, as a facilitator, instantly recognised and admired about her.

Through her genuine, sustained observations and personal experimentations with these practices, complemented by her humbling honesty about the barriers she faced in her own studies, Marie taught some illuminating sessions on meditation that totally clicked with me. Before I knew it, I was once again harvesting all that I could glean from my own practice to apply it to daily life. Marie brought each of her students a gift one day: a set of mala beads from India. The idea behind mala beads is that you hold each one for the duration of a breath, moving on to the next one only when you have finished the last breath. This sounds incredibly simple and yet was remarkably difficult to achieve.

Initially, I deliberately chose not to set a timeframe for my meditation sittings, instead opting to observe and record how long I could sit before distraction got the better of me. I would settle on the floor with my mala beads, set the stopwatch on my phone and concentrate on my breath. In the initial stages, I noticed how my brain and hand constantly raced onto the next bead and breath before the last was complete. I began to understand how this relates to the yogic philosophy of non-grasping-attachment, *Aparigraha*, one of the Yamas of Patanjali's Yoga Sutras. Each time I would reach for the next bead, I would check where the breath was and, when necessary, which was pretty frequently in the early days, I would re-adjust my hand and mind to the correct count. This was a delicate practice and training to slow down, to sit in the present moment no matter how strong or subtle the pull to reach for the next moment before it had arrived and to observe without judgement when I had once again grasped or raced ahead, as I would inevitably do.

This practice entirely changed how I could access new levels of patience, compassion and detachment from the external and internal environments; how I could be with the breath without the need for anything beyond that; how the quality of the breath would change the longer I sat with it. Breathwork and meditation are two very distinct practices. While they are wholly complimentary and even reciprocal, you soon realise that the quality of your meditation practice automatically influences the quality of your breath and vice versa. When you get to a point in your practice where you can surrender from the responsibility of doing *anything* except sit in stillness and awareness, cues like "How do you know you are breathing?" and "Can you let go of all tension and allow yourself to simply ***be breathed***?" really begin to illuminate how effortless some things can be, and just how much unnecessary friction we bring even to automated bodily functions, out of nothing more than a lack of conscious awareness. Particularly that second cue, "Can you be breathed?" When we study the breath from this perspective and relinquish control over it, observing without effort or precondition, we will see that even without our input, the breath still occurs. A common mistake in the early stages of meditation is that people, having been introduced to the concept of mindfulness and breathwork, think that controlling the breath and being aware of the rhythm of the breath as it enters and leaves the body are the same. They're not. As we've just considered, any ambition to be in control is a fool's errand, ultimately leading to some form of suffering.

Once that concept was locked in, it flicked on a series of other switches in my understanding. Never underestimate the value of nailing the basics!

I remember one distinct example of reaching this state through practice. I was lying in bed one night with my husband, feeling tired and frustrated that he was so deep in sleep and snoring loudly whilst I was wide awake and becoming increasingly more irritated by his grunts. I noticed that the more I focused on his snoring, the more irate the sound made me feel. My attention to this was fuelling the experience in a very negative way. I lay there in the dark and decided that I should have all the skills to get to sleep; after all, in yoga, we learn savasana or corpse pose, the relaxation piece at the end of most classes and, for a long time, I was entirely unable to get through this ten-minute practice without nodding off!

I corrected my posture in the bed to make myself comfortable and hoped I wouldn't have to move again during the practice. Then, I turned my awareness to my breath. First, I observed the qualities of my breath, and as it began to smooth out and soften, so did the muscles around my ribcage. To be clear, these were not commands nor instructions I was issuing to my body; this is simply a side effect of bringing your attention to rest on the breath and staying with it. I then noticed how this softening elicited deeper relaxation on a more global level throughout my body. I didn't expect what happened next, but to my surprise, the snoring began to sound like waves crashing against the shoreline. And I don't mean a vague resemblance in a half-dream-like state; I mean I felt transported to a specific place that I am very fond of, one which I often deliberately seek out for peace and contentment, only this time, it found me! I remember drifting off to sleep and thinking, "Wow, that right there is the power of meditation." Being able to convert your experience at any given moment despite external stresses and return to a calm, tranquil, restful state is a gift. Incredible!

Another landmark revelation for me in this practice was again experienced in bed. Once more, I was having difficulty getting to sleep, so I returned to focusing on my breath and observing the relaxation versus tension as it played out in my body. I had been practising for around ten minutes. All felt very calm and quiet; sleep was still just out of reach, but there was a serenity to the experience that felt restful, so I patiently savoured each breath as I lay cocooned by the stillness. Suddenly, without any warning or awareness from my thoughts or conscious mind, my body turned over in the bed. I lay there in the dark and thought, "Who's idea was that?" I wasn't clear on how this could happen, but I knew it did. My physical body just did something that neither my brain nor consciousness directed. Truth be told, it freaked me out a bit to know that my body could independently act on instructions when I didn't even know where or whom they came from, but another part of me was so intrigued that it was possible. Until now, I had never known the interconnected parts of my mind-body-soul so well. I was realising that they were distinguishable aspects of the same self. Yet, they were displayed as separate and perceivably autonomous, albeit invisible, shapeless entities.

It's common knowledge that the body moves out of harm's way through the nervous system signalling to the brain, usually long before our conscious awareness understands the danger. Think of the last time you burned yourself and how your body removed you from the danger before you realised you were even being burned. What surprised me about this instance was that there had been no stimuli, no danger. I didn't feel discomfort anywhere and certainly had no conscious intention to move even so much as a limb, let alone my whole self. So why the action? Was it habitual? Or was there something even more subtle at play?

I was beginning to see that many lessons I had learned throughout my yoga teacher training were appearing in other parts of my life and demonstrating how applicable and transferable these skills could be in everyday experiences. I was also beginning to understand how much of the wisdom I was so interested in seeking out had been hidden in plain sight this whole time. The basic fundamental principles shared with us from an early age are now interweaving to create a more nuanced and detailed tapestry of insight and overview.

I cannot say more fervently at this stage that rediscovering the basics in any practice is integral to our understanding of it. As we mature and evolve, we gain new, clearer perspectives, offering new revelations relating to old, fundamental principles.

Trigger warning: A cautionary note about guiding mindfulness practices, slowing down the breath and using a trauma-informed approach when teaching these topics to people whose background you don't know.

Many people don't realise that meditation practices and cues can be triggering in certain situations, so I feel duty-bound to bring that up here. When we are fortunate enough to be able to access states of relaxation and still feel safe in that space, then we may not be aware of the potential of causing distress for others, but if someone has faced any assault or violence, particularly at the hands of someone within their own home (and many perpetrators of violence are known to the survivors and victims), then lying still in complete silence may bring intrusive thoughts to mind. If they experienced intrusion and assault as they lay feeling safe in their bed, or if they were told to stay still or keep quiet, then often a cue to breathe slowly is enough of a trigger to establish similar enough physiological conditions that would bring up intense fear and trauma responses. Internationally acclaimed trauma expert *Dr Bessel van der Kolk, author of "The Body Keeps the Score"* describes how:

"Trauma is a visceral experience of heartbreak and gut wrench. When you are in your trauma [...] you don't know the difference between the past and the present because the timekeeper of your brain [the amygdala] goes offline, you lose all sense of perspective and whatever you are feeling is real, as opposed to feeling like a memory."

So, trauma is re-lived. It is experienced in the present moment each time it resurfaces. Therefore, to induce people into a state of relaxation which is believed to be appropriate and accessible for all, using generic cues and phrases, without any awareness for the potential and scope of how these experiences may replicate the conditions wherein a person experienced abuse, can at times catch the student and the teacher off guard.

Cues that I use when guiding practices include:

* * *

"Meditation may bring up some feelings of discomfort, which is entirely natural. However, some people can find these practices more distressing than beneficial, depending on previous experiences. If you become aware of something that you find triggering, I invite you to disengage from the practice and focus on gently moving your body in a way that feels safe for you. If you need to, please get up and move around the space. You can come speak to me about providing modifications, or regarding any other questions you may have"

"I invite you to close your eyes IF that feels safe and accessible for you today; otherwise, with eyes open, gaze softly at the floor in front of you"

"If you notice you are reacting with aversion to your experience in this moment or as we move further into the practice, feel free to blink your eyes open (or lift your gaze) and take a few moments to orientate yourself around the space. What can you see, hear, smell, feel?"

"This is not a 'no pain, no gain' situation. Please don't force yourself to 'push through' a practice if something feels unsafe or too challenging in this moment. Better that we prioritise self-compassion and safety."

"Trust your gut, nervous system and intuition. If this practice doesn't feel right for you, please speak to me or your teacher about it."

* * *

If you are in this situation as a participant and your instructor isn't offering such cues, know that neither of you is at fault. Trauma-informed approaches won't be a speciality for all teachers, but likewise, please know that you as the participant have done nothing wrong if you experience something triggering within these practices. It isn't something you've done or not done that has created these conditions. It isn't an inherent problem in your being a bad or unworthy person. It isn't that you should've said more or should've known better. As I mentioned before, defaulting to thoughts of "I thought I'd got past this" or "I should be over this by now" are not helpful in this situation and perpetuate the notion that *you* are inherently bad or flawed. You're not.

This will make more sense as we work through the following chapters, but perhaps distinguishing between guilt and shame is useful here. When we feel guilty, we can detach ourselves and our self-worth from the situation: "I feel bad about what I said to you when I was upset."

Shame occurs when we can't differentiate between an event and ourselves: "I am horrible for the things I've said."

Some researchers believe that shame is the emotion which converts most readily to trauma. That is why this distinction is so important. Your words, how you speak to yourself, how you interpret what other people say to you and how you use them to interact with others are of great importance. If you have advocacy to choose, be deliberate and intentional in your words. If you are at a point where you feel ill-equipped to articulate yourself, where externalising words aloud feels too dangerous (and I know what that's like - I've been there, too), then start by noticing your inner monologue. How do you speak to yourself? Whose views are they? Are these really your thoughts and beliefs, or is this something that has been projected onto you?

Chapter Seven
Vipassana

In February 2017, I went on a Goenka Vipassana retreat - ten days of silent meditation in a private centre, which they referred to as a compound. I had applied to attend these retreats a few times before, when they took place in Ireland and Britain, and could never secure a place. When I found out I was going to Sri Lanka on my honeymoon, I immediately looked to see if there were any Vipassana retreat centres there, and of course, there were plenty to choose from. I made my application, and within seventy-two hours, I had been offered a space.

Having cultivated a practice of opening up to timely and aligned experiences, despite how odd they might appear out of context, especially to onlookers, I have learned not to ignore when it feels like the universe is giving me a green light. Some call this *pronoia* - the opposite of paranoia - when the universe conspires in your favour.

I know attending a ten-day silent retreat on your honeymoon is more than a little unconventional. It wasn't like this was something Skinner and I would do together - meditation is not his thing. Still, I felt strongly compelled to take this path despite the external appearances, expectations, and societal constructs of convention. It seemed like the only reasonable thing to do. I will say that my husband does several things which I regard as his kind of meditation, and I guess this is a valuable tip for people who say they can't meditate. Indeed, it's one of the first things that I teach.

There is no such thing as "can't meditate," but everyone will have a different entry point. As with learning any new skill, if we can link it or relate it to something we already understand and enjoy, we can access it more readily. When Skinner describes his experience of swimming, for example, he speaks of it in the same terms that I would use to describe meditation: experiencing periods of serenity and calm, focusing on the breath, clearing the mind by directed attention on a single objective, achieving a more relaxed state through a monotonous practice, clarity on things that have been taking up thinking space in our minds, etc.

So, very often, it's not that you can't meditate, it's that you haven't found your hook, your way in, or that you haven't realised that one of your hobbies is essentially already a mindfulness-based meditation practice, as most people think this has to be done sitting stationary with your eyes closed, chanting. Coupled with that, there are many types of meditation that have distinctly different parameters because they teach different lessons. However, the more I have studied various types of meditation, the more I recognise that despite the lessons being different, the destination, i.e. the feeling you are working towards cultivating, is ultimately the same. This is beautifully demonstrated within Buddhist philosophy, which outlines the Noble Eightfold Path, i.e. that a commitment to living a life of service will eventually engender liberation from the manmade constructs which bind us in much the same way a seated meditation practice can, and that a deliberate cultivation of intention is of equal merit and efficacy to one of compassion. The activity in and of itself is not generally the determining factor; it is the devotion you bring to it that will yield results.

Skinner and I went to Sri Lanka for two weeks to celebrate our honeymoon, and after that, he flew home, and I made my way to the retreat centre. I arrived with all my luggage (I had packed to be in the country for a whole month), and I remember being met with smirks of "Look at that silly little white lady with all her worldly possessions," both from the locals who were there to volunteer for the retreat and from the other retreat attendees. I knew better than to allow that to annoy me, but I clocked it all the same.

The information and itinerary for the retreat weren't available online, so we waited tentatively to find out more about what to expect. We were corralled into a canteen-style area and given numbers to await our turn for registration. During registration, we were given our locker number and asked to hand over any phones, valuables, and any other distractions we might like to put out of arms' reach. We were also given a room number and the name of our roommate.

The ethos of these retreats is that you spend ten days turning more and more inwards whilst conversely tuning out the world around you. There is to be no talking, no eye contact or physical exercise, no eating outside of meal times, no reading, writing or other cognitive stimulation and no mixing between sexes. By abstaining from all stimuli, you can access the quietest corners of your awareness and begin to perceive new conditions and experiences of *self* beyond your typical day-to-day frame of reference.

Once I had completed registration, I went to my dorm room, which had two beds, each made of cast concrete plinths with 2cm thick foam mattresses. The room was very basic. There was half a thin curtain to obscure the doorway for privacy. Then, another full-length curtain divided the room. Aside from the beds, the room had a rickety ceiling fan, which gave a rather satisfying rhythmical clickety-clack as it spun well beyond a speed that sounded safe. Apart from that, there was a small window high up on the wall that looked straight into the jungle canopy beyond the compound perimeter. I took the bed closest to the door and began to unpack while I waited for my roommate's arrival.

So, what can you learn about yourself in ten days? Well, given that I didn't have the option to write or record anything for those ten days, when my belongings were returned to me, I quickly scrawled down a few notes, aiming to identify a key learning from each day to track what, if anything, had changed. I already knew it had. The word *Vipassana* means "to see things as they really are," and I could feel the layers of clouded vision, half-truths and unjustified, compound resentments dissolving away as I brought pen to paper for the first time in almost two weeks.

Before I describe the retreat, I would like to advise caution about consuming any and all information dished out by practitioners, teachers, and gurus. Indeed, please take anything I say with a pinch of salt and learn to critically interrogate everything others would sell as 'the truth.' Their truth is not the only truth.

In the early days, when we awaken to new truths or experience blissful practices, it can be easy, through excitement and eagerness, to consume whatever is put before us under the same banner. I have, across my many practices, met gatekeepers and self-professed guardians; those who would seek to belittle my efforts to maintain their perceived, elevated status. They scoffed with derision when I mentioned Vipassana or whatever else because perhaps they felt it made a mockery of their comparable years of practice and dedication.

This version of spiritual bypassing is particularly insidious. It is a perspective that originates from ego and is perpetuated by shaming the student, making them feel like they haven't tried hard enough or aren't committed enough for the long haul. The implication, even if it's not explicitly stated, is that the student is looking for a quick fix, a shortcut, and that they're lazy and only motivated by instant gratification. The irony is that this is precisely how our brains are wired to work. Check out *"Atomic Habits" by James Clear* to get a better sense of how your brain operates and how its job is to pursue solutions, finding the path of least resistance so that you can access those solutions or habits more organically in future without the need to expend vast amounts of energy each time.

Some immersive experiences, most especially if they are not facilitated by people who have gained expertise over many years, can sometimes, sadly, serve as little more than a tokenistic illusion of progress. At worst, they risk being detrimental to the participants' well-being, but you will find that with almost anything you might pursue these days. The rise of capitalism, consumerism, social media and digital and portable technologies means we must become ever more discerning in our choices and critical thinking. It's not necessarily the best teacher who becomes renowned for their work anymore, but the one who's best at marketing and search engine optimisation.

It's not that I attended this Vipassana retreat to suddenly experience a transformation and become enlightened instantly; far from it! It was just the best entry point for me at that level at that time. There was nothing remotely similar I could access in my locality, and I only had a short window of opportunity to explore.

Often, if an experience is in sufficiently stark contrast to how we usually live, there can be enough learning to make it valuable and, yes, even transformational. So, when you're on this journey, I urge you to cherry-pick which advice and comments you take on board. Notice when you feel locked out and try to recognise how, with whom or when that sensation first arose. Who's guarding the gate? And what are they trying to *control*? This approach often comes from a place of fear where feelings of inadequacy, insecurity and self-doubt are projected onto others.

Look up Brené Brown's explanation of avoiding "candle blower-outers" and "people who aren't in the arena regularly getting their asses kicked" to bolster your confidence on this topic specifically.

"Either you walk into your story and own your truth, or you live outside your story and hustle for your worthiness."
Brené Brown

The more you practise mindfulness, the more you may see that you, too, have done these things to other people. I have, I'm embarrassed to admit, mocked other singers who maybe hit a bum note, only to discover later that how I have judged others is often how I am silently critiquing myself on autopilot without even realising. I can remember hearing someone from a corporate background talk about their path to becoming a meditation teacher. They spoke about wanting to study mindfulness after a personal experience of its incredible benefits. When they said they searched for months to find the best course with the most prestigious qualification, backed by all the best research, I recall how I sneered silently at the thought.

The ego-led part of my mind began pointing out that their qualification was no match for my lived experience of the practices and, yes, you've guessed it. The longer I sat with this feeling, the more I realised that I was the one who was feeling insecure and inadequate without my certificates and conferred credibility, full of self-doubt, having never pursued the academic study of mindfulness meditation. As I caught these thoughts and simultaneously recognised that just because I thought them, it didn't mean I actually believed them, I learned a valuable lesson. I had just as much capacity and inclination to gatekeep as any of the people I'd met along my journey. Thankfully, I caught those nonsense curveballs before saying or actioning anything out loud, but this is the nature of mindfulness-based practices. There is always room to know yourself better. To be really honest with yourself and to discover new ways that your ego has been orchestrating your actions without your knowledge, let alone consent.

The day of arrival at the Vipassana retreat doesn't count as part of the ten-day experience, which I hadn't understood, so I came preparedly mute. On this day, you get set up, are shown around, and settled in. Then, after a light night's sleep, a large bell chimes at 4 a.m. to wake participants, and the course begins at 4.30 a.m. with a two-hour practice, or "sit," as it is often referred to, in the Meditation Hall.

Day One: "Your True Nature"

After the first night's sleep in my dorm, I awoke to find that I had been trapped under my mosquito net with at least one "mossie." I had over fifty bites across both my legs, and I'll admit I was a little unnerved by the fact that any one of those could've been from a dengue-spreading mosquito. Dengue is a deadly viral disease in Sri Lanka that we had learned about from the locals during our honeymoon.

I arose, dressed, and then set off up the small, steep hill to the Meditation Hall. It was beautifully tranquil at that time of the morning. There's a quality to the air that is so still, peaceful and spacious since most of the world is asleep, that it is a time of the day when I feel entirely at ease and wholly connected to my environment. I could describe myself as a nocturnal person, so comfortable am I at these times.

A two-hour sit is a challenge for anyone not well seasoned in their meditation practice, but with legs covered in itchy bites, it was a new level of distraction for me initially. Luckily, I had learned some years before, both on the Mongol Rally trip and when leading youth exchange programmes to Finland, that scratching these bites makes them exponentially itchier! I was so grateful to have had previous experience of ignoring the sensation of itch until it goes away, and so, for the duration of my first sit in the hall, I spent my time steering my attention away from the various sites of inflammation along my legs; I gently, diligently and repeatedly returned my awareness back to my breath.

The bell chimed to alert us to the end of the session. Then we were to make our way to the canteen for breakfast. I took my time walking down the hill as almost all the other meditators passed me by in a rush to cue up for food. I was delighted to have the opportunity to change gear from my normal 100-mile-per-hour lifestyle and intentionally sunk into a pilgrimage-style pace of observing each foot kiss the ground beneath it, like the mala beads practice, exploring each moment fully before letting it go to receive the next moment without grasping for it. I literally had nowhere else to be, and it was an incredibly novel experience in my life at that time to sense no urgency, be so anchored in the now, and feel like I could set down responsibility for everyone and everything.

I pulled up a chair for breakfast, which consisted of dhal, banana, and hot water. As I was gazing out the canteen window, I noticed a mosquito flying around the front of my face. I gently tried to wave it away several times, and it stopped.

I'll add here that since becoming a vegetarian, I have become absolute in my dedication to not inflict unnecessary harm against another being, to the point where swatting insects and terminating pests felt as barbaric to me as raising livestock solely for slaughter. So, I would never dream of swatting a mosquito. Through various previous encounters and conversations with people who live in countries where mosquitoes are prevalent, I learned that they can't bite if they can't land, so the most humane, effortless way to redirect a mosquito is either to simply blow them away or to keep moving.

When I noticed the buzzing had stopped, I looked down into my cup to find a mosquito floating on the surface. Previously, if I had spotted an insect in my drink, especially in a hot drink, I would've just thrown the contents of the cup away and replaced that drink with a fresh one. I mean, why would I want to drink mosquito tea? But this time, for whatever reason, I put my finger into the cup and caught the mosquito on my fingernail to fish it out. I brought that hand to rest on the table beside my plate, feeling incredibly uncomfortable at the idea of scraping the sodden insect off my nail, crushing its almost invisible, delicate wings to mere mush in the process. So, instead, I just continued to eat my breakfast. Some minutes later, I noticed another mosquito flying around the front of my face and happened to glance down at my fingernail. The soaking wet mosquito was gone. Perhaps this was the same one back to pester me again, who knows?

What I realised in that moment was my tendency to equate all life as equal, except for my own, and that I would sacrifice my own health and right to life to secure that of another. Moreover, I recognised that my actions were deeply grounded in compassion. I would not intentionally set out to hurt another, even if they have been the first to strike. A wry smile spread across my face as I understood that there was an imbalance here that I needed to address at some point. I wasn't quite sure where to begin with it, truth be told, but in becoming aware of it, I knew that I had taken the first step.

Later that evening, we were in the same canteen for two hours of discourse after some twelve hours of seated practice across that day, as is the format of Goenka's Vipassana. This first discourse explained how, in this practice, we would begin to realise our true nature, and again, a smile danced across my face as I acknowledged that I had indeed set off on that path. But my most humbling lesson that day was using a mosquito net. As I thought, you don't put the net down and keep it down all day to keep everything out. No. Instead, you keep the net pulled up out of the way during the day and bring it down when you go to bed, as there are much fewer mosquitos around outside of the hours of dusk, dawn, and daylight more generally. My previous attempt was more like mosquito-catching! I noted how fear had made me massively exaggerate the amount of intervention required, creating the situation I was actively trying to avoid.

I climbed into bed that night at about 9.30 pm and honestly couldn't remember the last time I had made it to bed so early. I was ready for Day Two, but I was also a little worried that I wasn't going to be cut out for this. I'm not usually one for doubting myself, but the seed was there, and I had no idea whether or not it would grow into an invasive species.

Day Two: "You are so loved"

The second day took my breath away in all kinds of ways. In one sense, I found it incredibly frustrating that the nuns, mentors, and even some volunteers who were there to guide, support, and facilitate our practice were asking questions of us, inviting us to speak, and, in the case of one particular volunteer, trying to entice us into having conversations about boys and soap-opera-style gossip with anyone who would listen. I found this a real challenge. As I mentioned before, fairness is one of my core values and within that is an inherent commitment to play by the rules. I get that not everyone sees rules the way I do and that I can be quite literal in my interpretation of social constructs. Still, when I attend a ten-day silent retreat and am told not to make eye contact, much less speak to anyone, the last thing I am expecting is to be brought into a group of practitioners and teachers to discuss aloud what we had covered that day.

As I was later reliably informed, this is not a common experience of Vipassana retreats; it was just this particular one I was on. It was no bad thing, as I learned as much about myself from observing my reaction to this as from anything else across the week. Sometimes, I'm too hard on other people; sometimes, I'm too hard on myself; sometimes, my expectations and desire for control cause friction where there doesn't need to be any. Most notably, I understood once more that the judgements I project onto others are the same judgements I allow to run unchecked within me, assaulting my self-esteem with Ninja-like stealth in the quietest recesses of my mind.

It's not like I was being scored on how well I did the retreat. When I initially discussed my plans to do the retreat with Skinner, I considered doing it as a charity fundraiser. He advised against it, telling me to do it for its worth and experience rather than tie it into some other type of external validation. I have to say, he was absolutely right, and I am always so grateful for his insights and balanced perspective, not least for his pragmatism in recognising when I'm trying to justify something that I feel like I need to do. Beware the trap of what I call "conferred credibility": "I'm a good person doing good things" – you might be and you can be, but this type of spiritual bypassing where you have to be (or at least pretend to be) all love and light, no shadows allowed, is a dangerous ego-driven perspective which gives out unrealistic benchmarks and keeps people entrenched in "I'm not worthy" mentality. Don't get me wrong, philanthropy and charitable pursuits are laudable, but when you get to a place where you believe your value and humanity is defined by how "good" you can be seen to be, or conversely, where you choose to stay away from pursuits you would like to engage with based on a notion that you're "not good enough" to dare try them, you've inadvertently prioritised other people's judgement over your own experience of, and potential for peace and contentment.

I can say without a shadow of a doubt that Skinner supports me in a way that I had never experienced outside of my family unit until I met him, despite having had many friends and relationships previously. Over the years, he has been one of my most prolific teachers regarding the practice of patience and understanding, alongside my parents.

The flip side of my frustration with the entirely unsolicited group chats I found myself involved in during the first two days of the silent retreat, was that I was equally blown away by our focus on meta meditation during seated practice that same day, i.e. sending out love, kindness and positive intention to those who might need it, through degrees of separation.

After the midday session, I sat outside the meditation hall and sobbed quietly but wholeheartedly. I wasn't trying to attract any attention, and I certainly didn't want to talk about it, but some of the volunteers, mostly local Sri Lankan women, gathered around me to make sure I was alright. I wiped away my tears, smiled as sincerely as I could, and bowed deeply to their kindness.

I think that day's discourse so moved me because it took me right back to being in Sally Taylor's yurt five years earlier. Whether you know it or not, whether you want it or not, there are people worldwide praying for you and your happiness. I use the word praying here in the broadest sense. If I could describe it in a secular way, it would be to say that people are sitting down to send good thoughts your way to counter the inevitable onslaught of negative thoughts which come from living without awareness. How beautiful is that?

It's funny. This weeping in a community where there was no common language, nor opportunity to communicate beyond what was visibly on show felt very nurturing, cathartic and just a huge relief, like the burden of being misunderstood no longer mattered because, for every person who would misunderstand me, there would be another complete stranger meditating for my happiness without ever knowing or questioning if I even deserved it. I was happy to cultivate and give unconditional love, but learning to receive that from anyone other than my husband or parents is where the real work started, and I have to say, I'm not there yet. However, people often comment on how I receive compliments with grace and presence rather than embarrassment, contraction and contradiction, as is often the case when we respond to such things without awareness, so I believe I am making progress on this!

Day Three: "Hitting a wall"

Other people's glass ceilings are not your glass ceilings, and vice versa. Goenka pointed out in the discourse at the end of Day Two that this was the day he struggled with the most, and in leading thousands of people through this process, Day Two was consistently the day that seemed to be the biggest hurdle for most people. For me, it came much later during Day Three. I was fine up until about lunchtime on Day Three, when I started getting this tickly cough in the back of my throat.

Practising meditation brings your awareness to all manner of distractions. I assumed that these distractions would all be thought-based, but as it happens, that's just one type of distraction. This cough was not, as I had initially interpreted it, an environmental symptom of my trauma-impacted asthmatic respiratory system but rather a psychosomatic manifestation of my ego trying to disrupt my learning in pursuit of universal truths.

At times throughout the day, during various sits of differing lengths and focuses, I would concern myself with how frustrating and distracting it must be for others to listen to me cough the whole way through our session. I would distract myself from my practice by forcing my ribcage to manage my breathing so as not to aggravate the incredibly sensitive tipping point between coughing and not coughing, and in so doing, I would not be focusing on observing the breath as it flowed naturally in and out of my body. Somehow, I had instead allowed my ego to take over and control the situation without my conscious mind being aware of it. It seemed as though the minute I unwittingly handed control over to my ego, it set the wheels in motion for a full-scale self-sabotage. I began to think of sugar-filled soothing throat lozenges that I had stowed in my rucksack and that maybe just one after-hours would be enough to get rid of this nuisance cough. As if!

That evening, during discourse, Goenka described how the ego did not want us to remain on this path as, ultimately, we would need to let go of it. Rather than the ego allowing this to happen easily, it would resist in all manner of ways by throwing up all kinds of distractions.

Once again, a knowing smile diffused across my face as the realisation sank in that this was precisely what I was experiencing earlier in the day with my cough and that even in the midst of these seemingly very real and lucid diversions, I was on the right track. I went to bed that night, settling into the knowledge that I did not have a cough, and I didn't cough for the remainder of the retreat - not once.

In the hustle and bustle of everyday life, it can be difficult to gain this level of granular insight into how we function. We often feel like we are forced to make reactionary decisions without adequate information or resourcing. We fail to recognise the competing priorities of the various strands of Self influencing our multiple outlooks, ambitions and aversions. We take a sweeping, superficial overview of any given situation and jump in with both feet, assuming that we know what is going on when, in reality, all we're doing is running away with ourselves, being carried by a current of judgement, prejudice and fear. This is the infinitely easier path, but it will never be the path of fulfilment, compassion, contentment, or enlightenment.

One of the most illuminating things I learned on this day was that the body and mind can play tricks on the soul, but the soul can patiently outlast the endurance of the other two if we choose to allow it. If you can master sitting long enough to hear the answers, you can out-sit the tiresome tricks of the monkey mind and the culturally distorted, often grossly misinterpreted signals of the body.

Day Four: "Failure is not the end of the story, and neither is success!"

This was the first day that it felt like we went beyond a regular meditation practice in that this was the first day when we were so attuned to our individual, internal environments without the constant distractions from outside that we were able to begin expanding on the practices in a more developed way. By expanding, what I mean is to home in on the microscopic detail of the practice to really start to unpack what lies beneath the din of all our mental baggage and emotional clutter. It occurred to me how this was actually the beginning of the retreat - that the first three days of *Anapana* (focusing on the breath, air coming in, air going out) had been necessary preparation to allow us to drop into these sensations with as much awareness and sensitivity as we could source.

This notion was echoed in our evening discourse, and I can honestly say that each day, I would experience a revelation regarding where that day's lesson would lead, and sure enough, that lesson would be explicitly described in the discourse later that same evening. It was hugely reassuring to know that I was understanding the lessons and even felt like I was ahead of the curve most days, and yet, it also felt like it went entirely against this practice to anticipate, celebrate and keep score. After all, one of the main elements of Vipassana meditation is to notice when you react with craving or aversion, as these are two sides of the same coin, i.e. feeling the need to move towards or away from something rather than knowing it will move of its own accord if you simply observe its rise and fall. For the remainder of the retreat, I vowed to practise equanimity, regardless of what might arise or how it might manifest.

During this day, I had my first tangible insight into the nature of our bodies and how they function in an energetic sense. We were sitting in the sweltering heat; I could feel the beads of sweat as they formed on my body and were pulled towards the ground by gravity, sometimes picking up other beads along the way, sometimes racing down to the ground, other times stop-starting. I had learned not to react and instead simply observed as these beads of perspiration darted and meandered across the surface layer of my skin. That's when I began to experience the most bizarre sensation of tiny electric shocks dancing across my body from head to toe. The longer I sat and observed this energy transmission across my largest organ, the more it blew my mind.

Had I not been participating in this Vipassana retreat in the middle of a tropical jungle, I would never have had access to this particular experience. I was sure that the water from perspiration made the current of electricity so tangible and traceable. It was utterly fascinating to observe, most especially as I was someone who'd spent a considerable portion of my young adult life aiming to be, and believing myself to be more or less invisible and unremarkable. Somehow, this revelation of energy exchange made me understand how volatile we really are in our biochemical existence and how readily we conduct energy, both within ourselves and between people. That this was so obvious to me in these sensations and that we are usually totally blind to this in our everyday lives, was what sent my mind into a spin.

I've always known that I'm good at feeling and sensing energy. I can taste the atmosphere in any room I walk into, and I know when a person's intention towards me has changed before I've even looked at or spoken to them. I can smell the rain coming and tell when it'll fall, accurate to seconds, without looking at the sky. So, little about this observation surprised me when I really sat and thought about it, but it did highlight for me just how our constantly distracted, stretched, and overloaded senses have lost and forfeited many of our innate and, frankly, essential human qualities.

At the risk of repeating myself, it feels like we have inadvertently sacrificed so much of what it is to be human in the pursuit of civilisation. How is it that we have become more concerned about the quality of relationships between our favourite tv characters, yet when it comes to cultivating our own skills and abilities to read people, situations and environments with the most remarkable set of instruments that have ever existed, the human body and soul, we have willingly handed over our toolkit and reference notes in a trade-off for mind-numbing, soul-sucking engagement in the superficial?

As I sat on Day Four of the retreat in thunderbolt pose, a pose I had studied for years before in my yoga teacher training, I ached and squirmed and tried to manage the painful sensations in my body. The more I tried to force myself to sit as I knew how to do, the more my body gave off signals of pain, discomfort and outright unwillingness to comply. The main lesson here was that bodies are fluid, in a structure and capacity sense, from moment to moment, day to day. Just because I can touch my toes one day doesn't mean I'll be able to access the same privilege the next day. Just because I knew I could comfortably sit in thunderbolt pose from previous experience, it didn't mean I could access it unhindered in that particular set of circumstances.

Truth be told, by this point, my whole body was giving off various aches and niggles; the area between my shoulder blades hurt from trying to sit upright with good posture for fourteen hours a day, my back hurt from sleeping on concrete, my hips were sore from sitting in a cross-legged pose, so I thought "Yes! Thunderbolt pose could be the ideal solution here." An effortless way to stack my shoulders above my hips and take all the weight and strain out of my back. I could barely sit for longer than ten to fifteen minutes without getting restless and wanting to move, but by this point in the retreat, you are encouraged not to move at all, no matter the appeal or impulse to adjust. I observed the thoughts of moving as they arose and gently let them pass without getting too involved. Pretty soon, the muscles in my legs began to feel like they were on fire. After the previous day's coughing lessons, I resolved to stay put for the duration of the sit, no matter how much the sensations pressed me to do otherwise. Each time I was drawn into the sensation, I would see how long I could stay there without reacting until it either passed or changed. Sometimes the sensations would subside, sometimes they would move, and sometimes I would get distracted by something else entirely. There were occasions, however, where the sensations became so dull and insipid that I could only have been observing from the third place of equanimity, as opposed to craving or aversion, which was a staggeringly unique vantage point!

For these bodily sensations to be so ferociously all-consuming one minute, only to transform into barely the ripple of a breeze on an otherwise tranquil lake the next, was quite eye-opening in terms of quantifying the amount of time, energy and friction we often bring to situations which we pre-emptively enter into with aversion, and how, very often, it is the friction and aversion that we bring to a situation which causes the most damage. Just like having breakfast in Turkey with the wasps or trapping the mosquitos in bed with me!

Practising the art of surrender and letting go would become one of my main learning points from this retreat. It would introduce me to the concept that the perceived amplitude of pain directly correlates to our capacity for stress management across our body, mind and spirit. I didn't know it yet, but armed with these remarkable experiences, this was a construct I would review some years later through an entirely different lens.

But for now, I was resigned to accommodating my discomfort in whatever way I could. I would sleep with a towel rolled into a long cylinder shape to place under my spine, which allowed my shoulder blades to fall on either side of it and undo the forward rounding that my shoulders were repeatedly slumping into during these long sits. As I began to interpret and understand the discourse of energy, intention and attention, I learned how to sit with discomfort until it would dissolve. We would practise this again and again over the coming days in a variety of formats.

Day Five: "It's a jungle out there!"

Everything rises to fall, and in the case of my most recent experiences, inevitably, you'll have to fall in order to rise.

As I diligently wandered my way around the compound, I began to observe how others had slowed their walking pace to match mine. I noticed how some people had observed me do simple things like setting out chairs for our teachers before they would arrive in the room or wearing their watch around their water flask rather than around a sweaty wrist. Over the course of the retreat, I noticed how I comfortably and causally led, even without the use of words or eye contact, commanding a relaxed sense of authority. I noticed how people would watch what I did and alter their conduct accordingly. I was surprised to see it at first and soon after, realised that on some level, I have always known that I'm a natural leader.

So I made my way around the tiny compound as though I were moving in slow motion, trying to take in all the sights, sounds and smells as if for the first time. It was a rather curious and conflicted experience to be at a silent retreat in the middle of a Caribbean island, and yet nearby, the noise of enormous, old diesel engines would be roaring through the streets; the churning rumble of their passing left ringing in the hills long after they'd gone; then, later, to feel how this intense backing track to the experience seemed to dull into nothing more than a gentle hum after a few days.

As I made my way back up to the mediation hall for our afternoon session, I remember gazing up into the canopy of giant tropical trees above my head just in time to see a huge, variegated, spade-shaped leaf gently drift its way towards the forest floor and then there it was; seeing it as if for the first time, the leaf landed softly and silently, resting amongst the rest of the decaying debris which had fallen from the trees. It was autumn here, after all, and as I scanned the undergrowth, marvelling at this sense of decay being nothing more than a cyclical part of life, I began to spot these tiny, lime-green shoots poking gingerly out of the black mulch of natural compost. These little shoots were like stars in the sky; the longer I looked, the more I could see. Hundreds of little antennae of hope were bursting forth to pursue growth, change and stretch.

At that moment, I felt like I truly understood the inevitability of balance that can be found between the swinging pendulum of life experiences; the predictability of a spring that follows even the coldest, most hostile winter, the circle of life that many of us strive to contribute to or impact in some meaningful way; even though ultimately life will roll on with or without us. There was something about experiencing the magic of our existence juxtaposed with its apparent irrelevance that was oddly comforting. You might as well do what makes you happy in life. There are no prizes for being a martyr.

"None of us are getting out of here alive, so please stop treating yourself like an afterthought. Eat the delicious food. Walk in the sunshine. Jump in the ocean. Say the truth you're carrying in your heart like a hidden treasure. Be silly. Be kind. Be weird. There's no time for anything else." *Nanea Hoffman*

Day Six: "Misery loves company"

The surprising solace in a single cell. I've already mentioned my inherent interest in fairness, keeping to the rules and diligently practising non-judgement - you can see how these two agendas may cause conflict. This was never more tested than the day I temporarily moved into a dorm with someone who saw rules as more like guidelines, someone who believed that everything was open to interpretation, and someone who prioritised their own wants and needs above that of the collective effort or any contract they'd freely entered into.

My roommate, for the duration of the retreat, was struggling with the imposed chronic lack of stimulation and would regularly go back to our room to knock out a few sets of High-Intensity Interval Training when no one was looking. If you don't know what this is, just search "HIIT workout" online, and you'll soon see. It's the energetic action that generates heat, sweat and buzz. Not only was this obvious from my roommate, the difference in her demeanour from before and after her workouts, but also from the energy I could feel when I entered the room. It was a strange sensation to walk into an empty room and feel able to sense that someone had been there not long before and had been moving frantically. That frequency had been in some way stamped onto the atmosphere so that I could perceive of and interpret it, even though I wasn't there to see it or 'know' it through my usual visual or auditory senses.

As the days went on, I saw that my roommate's movements were becoming quicker and jerkier. She began missing mediation sessions and, at one point, was even running up and down the compound in plain sight, an absolute "no-no" in terms of the code of conduct they ask you to sign up to before the retreat, which they then emphasise again at registration. Clearly, she was having difficulty.

We had heard in discourse one evening about how, when they taught Vipassana in the prisons in India, the inmates frequently could not sit still for the first few days. They would visibly jump and hop off the spot as they grappled with the many voices and judgements hiding in their minds and muscles. I hadn't seen much of this in our meditation hall, and other than my roommate, everyone else seemed to be coping alright, or so I thought. When we came to the final day, it appeared that anywhere between one-third and half of the original intake had left early, unable to complete the ten-day stretch.

I went back and forth for days in my mind. Should I speak to her? I could probably help. What is the right thing to do here? Eventually, I settled on the notion that if it had been any other circumstance, any other time, I'd have broken my silence and sought to support her. But this time, I decided to prioritise myself. Having realised earlier in the week that this is not my default mode, it felt like an opportunity to practise something different based on what I had observed on Day One with the mosquito.

When my roommate came to me on Day Six and told me she was leaving, I was totally overcome with guilt. I felt like I had let her down, that somehow, I was responsible for her happiness and capacity to succeed. Upon her admitting defeat, it took all the patience and self-compassion I could muster to tell myself and believe that I wasn't there to make her experience more palatable or hold anyone's hand. I had travelled to the other side of the world to participate in this relatively short opportunity, and I should focus on my practice to the exclusion of all distractions, no matter how uncomfortable. And yet, my mind raced with emotion as she explained that she was packed up, leaving and very glad to be doing so.

I didn't speak. I cried a little and walked her to the gate of the compound, helping her carry her bags. As I made my way back up to my dorm, I was surprised to feel like I could rest more easily. I'd been entirely unaware of how much mental and emotional strain it had been to share space with one other person until they were no longer there. Suddenly, I felt lighter, more relaxed and less apprehensive. It hadn't registered with me that I had been harbouring this tension until the feeling was no longer there. I went about the rest of my day, and as I relaxed into the utter solitude in my dorm that evening, I breathed a huge, unmistakable sigh of relief.

My lesson here was just how much mental, emotional and physical tension it takes to hold yourself together for other people. Even if they are total strangers or you don't feel like you owe them anything, you'll likely still exert some effort to mind your manners, be aware of fair boundaries, and navigate your way around them with minimal conflict. Perhaps I have a more honed and heightened sense of this, overdeveloped from growing up in a post-violent-conflict region, or perhaps we all perceive this the same way, and it just dulls over time when we don't need to draw on it daily for our own safety and preservation.

I can say conclusively that I felt better about it when she left. I am very well aware of my need for solitude to decompress, but I was surprised by just how much effort it took for me to create and manage that boundary. My scope to engage with her was entirely inhibited, even though I didn't have all the other typical day-to-day distractions and relationships to contend with.

Day Seven: "You're doing it all wrong.

You have three choices: react, ignore, or observe. Your brain will digest according to what you feed it. Be patient, happy, and grateful.

As I settled into the dorm on my own and observed how yesterday's events had generated emotion in me, I realised that even this sense of judgement, relief, etc, was all still the same thing. What I mean by that is, it doesn't matter which way the pendulum swings; if you are either happy or sad solely based on a set of external circumstances beyond your control, then you are still at the mercy of your monkey mind and running the risk of your happiness being entirely dependent on favourable external conditions.

Reacting to anything is normal and automatic, but choosing how to react is entirely skill-based, so it can be learned and trained. I can say with absolute certainty that when things have happened in the past, and I have given way to negative thoughts, this quality of thought has continued to bubble up and overtake me. Similarly, when taking an optimistic outlook, reactions generally continue along this trajectory. But the third option, to just observe, is a tricky one, not least because it requires you to understand how the ego orchestrates so much of what we do. We can believe we are a particular type of person for years, only to find that many of our behaviours can be attributed to aversions or cravings which we've developed in response to our experiences and the people in our lives. We are so much more than we think, and we can only begin to realise this when we learn to observe without judgement. If we can first learn not to react, there is an abundance of healing in this work.

Day Eight: "Waiter, there's a fly in my soup"

... or ant in my salad. It was too painful to look, not for the ant, it was quite happy.

As mentioned before, I have been a vegetarian for at least twice as long as I haven't been, and for over twenty years at this point. Within that, I felt that I had lost a sense of balance in the normalcy of life and co-existing on this planet. When I looked down and found half an ant on my plate amongst my lunch, I was immediately turned off; I felt crushed and creeped out.

Not so much by the idea of eating an ant, more reeling from the notion of this cruel and dramatic ending for the ant. Of course, I also wondered if other ants were hiding in my lunch, but primarily, I was upset for the ant. That was until I pulled myself away from these thoughts and looked back at my plate to find that the half-ant was gone. It had moved all by itself! I didn't understand how that would be possible, but it was, happening right before me. I learned in that moment that while I was breaking my heart over others, something I've watched my mother rehearse throughout my life, the ant or "victim" as I had come to regard it, got up and walked off! To know that my bleeding heart did absolutely nothing to help the ant and to find that, ultimately, it didn't even need my help or concern, was a real and very welcome wake-up call! My suffering over this ant was entirely ineffective and self-inflicted. All I was doing was torturing myself. Well, that's a metaphor for life if ever I'd heard one!

Something else I observed on this day was thinking I could hear music. By this stage, I felt like I knew the area where we were staying simply by its sounds and smells. For example, I knew that not long before nightfall, someone would light a fire just over the compound wall and stay there with it until daybreak. I knew that the trucks began to drive on the roads from around 5.30 am, and I knew the school bells would chime at various intervals through the day, followed by the bustling, playing and chattering of people going about their business somewhere in the distance. With the smell of perfumed soap and shower gel wafting through the air, I knew some of our participants were doing their laundry and personal hygiene routines outside the designated times. What I could pick up when I tuned into the environment was remarkable.

But there was this one sound that I couldn't quite place. Every now and again, I could hear stringed instruments playing in harmony. Each time I tried to identify or locate it during the breaks between our seated meditation sessions, it stopped, but when I relaxed and forgot about it, there it was again. I wasn't familiar with the melody, nor could I hear it well enough to identify the instruments, but I could hear music from somewhere. I decided it must be music playing from a local building in a village nearby. Still, the frequency and familiarity of the sound throughout the last few days of the retreat led me to believe otherwise. I started to imagine that this was the sound of my cells vibrating. My body was singing to me when I was still and quiet enough! Once more, I was floored with a deeply profound wonder of how incredible we are, not only as people, thinking, feeling, moving, doing, beings, but as vibrating instruments, vessels of art and awe.

Music resonated at a level deeper than anything else I could perceive across the duration of the retreat, and I wondered when my life soundtrack got put on pause. I remember, as a young person, I was always singing and expressing myself musically, and then somehow, for whatever reason that I wasn't consciously aware of at the time, it all stopped. Also, between my teenage years and mid-twenties, I had grown a debilitating aversion to singing, performing or any other form of eliciting attention.

Through this experience, I realised that my aversion to being visible, entertaining and engaging in playful, creative endeavours ceased when my breasts started to grow. That was when I began to express a preference for being invisible. No doubt any woman reading this will at least be familiar with that sentiment, if not for the first time realising why she also opted to become less visible at a similar age. This was a revelation that I'd had inklings about before and had moved to address unknowingly several times through signing up to various choirs and community music projects, but in this new understanding of how music is such an integral part of me, of us, I earmarked it as something I would dedicate time and effort to explore further after the retreat.

Day Nine: "Know Thyself"

I mentioned my "hanger" issues earlier, and the meal schedule for the retreat was something that I had anticipated would be a challenge. If it was your first time on retreat, you were offered breakfast, lunch and tea, i.e. fruit and a drink. You were supposed to skip tea if it was not your first time, but that bit wasn't enforced. Initially, I thought this was pretty hardcore, and I couldn't fathom how that might work, let alone why anyone would want to punish themselves in that way. However, as the days passed, I understood how, in slowing down to a snail's pace and doing little to no physical work, we didn't even need dinner or breakfast.

At the beginning of the retreat, I was going up for seconds at breakfast time, believing it to be the most important meal of the day. As the days rolled by, I went from having seconds to choosing a smaller plate, to ensuring that I went last in the line for food, knowing that the option for a variety of foods would be limited and the opportunity to access a full plate, seconds, or preferences for comfort foods would be diminished. I watched as others around me continued to race to the meal hall day after day at the end of each sit and scurry up two, sometimes even three times, to reload their plate, distracting themselves from what their bodies were trying to tell them.

I began to loosen my grip on my desire for food and instead observed how little I needed to fuel effective function. Compared to how much I ate on a typical day, I was blown away by the vast difference between these two quantities. This was my introduction to understanding how one might be able to function well whilst fasting, something I had spoken at length about with my friend but was yet to try by this point.

Another thing that had become so clear at this point was the distinct lack of physical pain and discomfort from the long sits and the hard sleeping surfaces. I no longer needed to sleep on a rolled-up towel. I could actively target areas of physical discomfort by simply sending my attention there to disperse the sensation through vibrational diffusion. Slowly but surely, I was learning to decipher the difference between my mental, emotional, physical and spiritual states as separate and often competing entities.

Day Ten: "Silence is golden"

... but a surprise phone call to a loved one on the other side of the planet has to be one of life's greatest gifts.

I was expecting Day Ten to be like the nine days before, and I got up as usual to spend the day immersed in meditation. After our two-hour sit in the hall, we were invited for breakfast, after which we were given back our belongings and told how the rest of the day would look. It was such an odd experience to go from living in absolute silence with a group of people to hearing the buzz and flurry of conversations, international accents and laughter flying around the compound.

A few people approached me directly to speak with me, mostly commenting on how relaxed I looked throughout the retreat. They asked how many of these I had done before, and some even said they were sure they had seen me at other retreats in Sri Lanka and different countries. One girl, Natalia, came up to me and said, "Yeah, I watched you walk around and thought, 'There's a girl who doesn't give a damn what anyone else thinks'" which didn't seem unusual to me until I realised that this is absolutely not how I felt about singing, so why is that one thing so different? Once again, I promised myself to revisit this disparity and committed to resolving this friction.

I took my stuff to my room and got my ukulele out of its case. I played some songs and warmed up the voice I hadn't used in over a week. It was still only 7 am in Sri Lanka, so it was far too early to make a phone call home as it would've been maybe 2.30 am there. I sang a few songs, and people stopped by my dorm to listen and tell me how beautiful my voice was. They were quickly followed by a nun who scolded me and told me I had a lot of work to do and that singing was not permitted. She ushered me into the shared toilets and showers to get on with cleaning. I was a little wounded by her curt reprimand but equally determined not to let it derail me. I set about cleaning as joyfully as possible, even though I was the only one working in the shared bathrooms.

After lunch, I took my phone out to the side of the compound and sat on the balcony to call Skinner. He answered the phone, and hearing the sound of his voice, and feeling like he was right there beside me took my breath away. I tried to speak, but nothing came out - no sound at all. He said my name a couple of times, and I could feel his anxiety and worry for my welfare rise slightly in the silence that he received back. I cleared my throat and tried again, but once more, nothing came out. Overcome by emotion and a mild sense of panic that he'd think something terrible had happened, I burst into floods of tears, knowing instantly that this was not what he needed to hear, but at least there was finally sound. I croaked, "I'm okay," in a barely audible and surprisingly high-pitched whimper, and he laughed and waited. I said again, "I'm okay," and cleared my throat. "It's so good to hear your voice," I said to him, and he began to talk while I gathered myself. He laughed softly as he gently held space for me to communicate with him. I told him about singing and the nun telling me off. He laughed again, knowing that such a thing would previously have been my worst nightmare and knowing that I sounded different about how little it had affected me this time.

I talked him through some of the things I had thought and seen and told him how much I missed him and was looking forward to seeing him when I got home in a few days. He told me how he had suddenly realised after I dropped him off at the airport on my way to the retreat that he had no way of finding me other than the photo he had taken of the taxi's licence plate. He had a fleeting concern as he waited for his plane home that he might never see me again, that my taxi could've taken me anywhere, and that he wouldn't have had any clue where to begin looking. I had organised the taxi for the airport run and then on to the retreat, so he wouldn't have had a contact number to follow up with if he hadn't heard from me after ten days.

We laughed about the oddity of our situation and how it was typical for us to be so relaxed about things other people might not dare allow themselves to experience. He told me about returning to work after the honeymoon and being met with questions like, "What do you mean your wife is still there? And you let her stay? What will you do if she decides not to return home?" Again, we laughed at the idea that marriage for some people means control, and we each knew that meeting on the far side of these kinds of experiences ultimately made us stronger as a couple. We weren't together through habit, obligation, or need. We have always been together through choice, conscious decision-making, and a commitment to remain paired through our growth and evolution.

After that short call, the meditators were summoned once again to the Meditation Hall for a final sit, and it was the most effortless and relaxed practice of the entire retreat. All the weight of expectation, hope and effort fell away to reveal a weightless, timeless suspension in nothingness. It felt like I had only just closed my eyes when the bell rang to announce the end of the session. I had several sessions like this during the retreat, and this one felt distinctly lighter and limitless.

No matter what you practise, if you don't succeed at first, aim not to be too hard on yourself. Wait until you feel resourced enough to try again. The last attempt will be worth the wait!

"Anicca" is a word that was used consistently throughout the retreat, much like how the ringing of a gong can act as a touchstone, reference point or anchor in a meditation practice, throughout the discourse we would be reminded of the Buddhist principle of impermanence through the sporadic use of the word "*Anicca*" (an-e-cha)

When I left the compound, it was a conscious decision to return home. Yes, that was the original plan, but having experienced the uncomplicated, illuminating and, at times, blissfully beautiful life of devotion, it could be easy to reconsider former plans in lieu of life at a monastery. Truth be told, I think my parents weren't entirely convinced that I'd return, but I was never more clear in my decisions; to live in my dharma, my truth, was to return to where I belonged; to share what I'd known and create opportunities for others to engage with these learning practices. I've never seen myself as a scholar of meditation like the monks or the academics. I see myself more as learning as I go, taking bite-sized snacks when I can, and inviting fellow adventurers to the table to share stories and food.

Committing yourself to a life of devotion might be your path, and if it is, good for you! If you do choose that option, please know that you will inevitably still face conflict and friction, since they are largely generated internally, inside yourself. You can still access noble truths and universal principles without committing to a monastery. It might take longer, and you'll likely become distracted, but if you choose life in all its chaotic, unpredictable and untamed glory, these are the trade-offs.

Chapter Eight

Shame & the Voice

How I found myself in Sri Lanka in the first place is another unconventional take on following a feeling contrary to the societal norms of perceived, appropriate conduct or rational thought.

When we married, we never considered Sri Lanka as a honeymoon destination. All we knew was that we would get married in a Big Top circus tent in the field beside our house, have a short break in Portugal for a few days after the wedding, and then we would have our proper honeymoon six months later. We agreed that we didn't want a five-star all-inclusive resort experience, so we looked at options like Cambodia and India. We realised that since we both worked in the charity sector, we didn't want to spend our honeymoon surrounded by abject poverty, feeling guilt-ridden and obnoxious. We wanted to spend our time together without any unnecessary emotional torture.

Between getting married and going on my honeymoon, I was introduced to a musician called Julius Mitchell through a Belfast-based charity I worked with called Beyond Skin. Julius was visiting Northern Ireland on a couple of occasions throughout the summer of 2016, and during this time, my family experienced a bereavement which shook me to my very core. Between Julius' first and second visits, my outlook, my mental health and my interest in life had imploded. And yet, somehow, we ended up forming a bond that, to this day, is one of the most meaningful and authentic connections I've ever known.

I describe meeting Julius and hearing him sing as a sound so pure that it reached me through a darkness impervious to almost anything else. The second time he returned to Northern Ireland, I was actually out of work on sick leave due to my consuming encounter with grief. So we spent days together, walking, singing, and talking. I noticed the mental friction that I came up against over and over again when I was invited to sing along. I continually tried to soften around it, pushing myself to find a way, but it was relentless and defiant. I told him when we first met that I didn't sing, and he snorted this grunt of disbelief before bursting into laughter. He said, "Róisín, if I didn't understand English, I'd think you're singing to me all the time, the way you talk." And sure enough, when I thought about it, I realised that I have a very animated, textured prosody, and to hear me say, "I don't sing," must have sounded so incredulously absurd.

When he left for London, he invited me to go with him for a few days, and I did. I spent some time meeting with other artists, and going to open mics - I even sang at a few of them, and, despite being awfully out of tune and devastatingly mediocre, I felt a huge sense of relief that I was finally starting to make my way out of the shame-filled hole I'd found myself in regarding my relationship with my voice. I didn't realise it then, but some of my work environments added to my shut-down response around authentic expression. They didn't feel safe, mostly because I'd witnessed firsthand how people's kind words and good deeds were distorted, manipulated, and used as weapons against them.

I was so lucky to meet Julius when I did. If you are lucky enough to meet people who are relentlessly patient and kind to you, you'll have everything that you are reflected back to you better than any glass mirror ever could. This is an incredible gift and blessing.

At this point, I was deaf in one ear and had been for several months, which was inexplicable by any of the doctors I had seen. I later came to understand it as a stress-induced illness, a psychosomatic symptom of the toxic conditions I was repeatedly in over a sustained period of time. I didn't know what sound therapy was at this point, but I knew that his frequency was safe, therapeutic, and wholly nourishing, even in silence. It cast stark, contrasting shadows onto the vindictive, poisonous and destructive contexts I had otherwise been immersed in. I should say that Beyond Skin was one of the only places I worked during this time, which was contrary to this experience. A beacon of light in what felt like an otherwise shady existence.

So I came home from London and did more open mics in Belfast bars. I sang in the park, and I played in front of my friends, which just a few short months before, at my wedding, had seemed entirely unachievable, let alone enjoyable! Before I knew it, one of my musician friends asked me to play as a warm-up act at their show night, a paid gig as a solo musician in my own right, on the same lineup as musicians I thoroughly admired and respected. I couldn't believe it!

Of course, I said yes! I took to the stage, and I sang my heart out. I fluffed chords and fell out of key, but I fumbled through that performance, after which I hugged the same pint of beer for nearly two hours! I found this detail especially weird because I expected to knock back some celebratory drinks in my first-ever post-gig afterparty as a solo entertainer. I'd been to many afterparties, but never as a solo artist. Little did I know, my disinterest in alcohol that night was actually due to my being pregnant. Within weeks of realising that I was growing a tiny human in my tummy, I left all my jobs, voluntary roles and anything else which I felt might be too toxic to risk exposing my unborn child to.

This massively oversimplifies how the next few months panned out, so in the next story, I'll circle back and talk about the devastating family bereavement I mentioned earlier. But first, it's worth noting that none of these paths were easy; none of these decisions just happened without conscious effort or consequence. Each time I chose to follow a path that had no obvious reason or signposts, it took a great deal of faith and resolve to continue moving forward based on nothing more than my gut feeling.

Much like your vocal cords and muscle body, your intuition can be developed with dedicated, progressive training. I see our intuition as a mix of information between the environmental safety cues we receive through our Vagus Nerve (which terminates in the gut, hence the term "gut feeling"), our memory of previous, similar incidents that will inform our frame of reference, and our conscious awareness of the other invisible factors which might be at play such contextual, historical and psycho-social information that generally informs expectations around predictable behaviour. Therefore, we train our intuition by understanding that these strands of information interact and interplay and by addressing each one separately.

Training the Vagus nerve requires stimulating and regulating the vagal tone, which can be done through various activities and modalities such as breathwork, singing or chanting, tapping, sound therapy, massage, cold exposure, auricular acupuncture, exercise - the list goes on and on. Regulating the tone of your Vagus nerve will create conditions for it to perceive your environment more accurately and decipher safety cues.

Training our memory of similar events requires us to apply critical thinking. I know that my memories carry an emotional signature or time stamp from the experience. However, as time moves away from the experience, and through the practice of meditation, we have an opportunity to reinterpret these experiences without bias or judgement, which allows us to 'file' that information in a more appropriate way.

Finally, conscious awareness of other influences comes down to education, formal or informal. Read books, study topics you're interested in, listen to podcasts, talk to people from different backgrounds, and travel! These experiences will inform your worldview and give you extra data to work with when trying to conclude what is going on in any situation.

In taking up singing again, I learned how to self-regulate my own traumatic incidents. I spent time observing how my body reacted in various musical contexts and circumstances in much the same way I approached understanding my reaction to hugs. I learned how to identify and correct the many distortions I had clung to over the years regarding music, singing and my capacity for creative expression. I noticed that my reluctance to sing in public was anchored in a sense of shame that I had accumulated over time about my voice; not only whether or not I was a good singer but also in relation to the things I thought were appropriate to say. I realised that I believed my voice to be the main expression of my identity, and I genuinely didn't have anything nice to say about it. This realisation highlighted one of the many lies I had told myself. How could I go from performing fearlessly as a principal character in musical productions in front of hundreds to this - without even noticing?

Through Beyond Skin, I heard about a guy called Dr Ahmad Sarmast, the Director of the Women's Afghani Choir. Dr Ahmad was a named priority target on the Taliban hit list, cited as dangerous for giving women access to singing, instruments, and hope through music. Whenever the Taliban took control in Afghanistan, they entirely banned listening to, learning and playing music. Dr Ahmad's women's choir faced similar threats, too, and were all ostracised from their families and communities for choosing to participate in music. I realised how privileged I was. I mean, here were these young women, risking life and limb just to be able to sing, and here I was, with all the access and opportunity in the world, and yet

I felt wholly incapable of participating, but I persevered. I sang through the screechy, crackly bits, uploaded videos of my singing to social media, played any gig I was offered, and began to run my own open mic nights, creating a community where other people could tackle their fears in a safe and nurturing environment, just like I had done. I started several community music projects, got involved with Girls Rock School NI, and even fronted a three-piece band for a while. At times, I barely recognised myself or the life I had created; it was all centred around the desire for true connection to myself and others.

When the 2020 pandemic lockdowns happened, there were no more singing groups. No more performances. But I didn't let that stop me. I took my work online and regarded it as one of the most necessary pieces of work I had ever done, especially at this time of extreme isolation and disconnection. I thought that meditation and yoga would be my most in-demand modalities, and while these online classes attracted attention, no one was more surprised than me to discover that what the majority of people needed from me was my music, my presence and my fearlessness in the face of change.

One of my favourite projects was a community music project with a group of Syrian refugee women. We met weekly on Zoom, chatted and sang a few songs. It wasn't long before these women opened up about some of the traumatic incidents that led them to flee their homelands. Singing relieved internal, pent-up pressure for these women, allowing them to relax and speak more freely. I felt the importance of what my facial expressions conveyed as the translator spoke between us. Smiling, singing and consciously not frowning even when the stories felt heavy, all contributed to creating the environment that brought healing and helped these women alleviate traumas stored in their bodies for years. I felt so honoured to do this work and to develop a personal connection to these women and their stories of conflict, trauma, and resilience.

Over the years, I have found many examples of this, where creating space and giving permission for others to express themselves vocally has been transformational and healing. I speak more about shame and the voice again in Chapter Sixteen, "Being seen, heard, and felt."

Chapter Nine

About Grief

Brené Brown is a *Grounded Theory* researcher who collects stories and analyses the patterns across many contributors' lived experiences. She is one of my favourite people to listen to regarding the human experience, not least for her early work on women and shame. Much like my yoga teacher, she is wildly honest and authentic. She's so real, you can't help but like her. Her work speaks for itself and often requires her to reconsider her own biased positions and perspectives within the context of all the data she collects. In the way she shows up and models vulnerability, informed by her research, she invites us to gently peel back the layers of what we think we believe so that we can understand ourselves better through the lenses of courage, vulnerability, shame and empathy.

She talks about *creativity scars* as something that was identified in over half of the sample interviewees during their experience of arts participation in schools. They experienced incidents relating to their artistic ability that were so shaming that they changed how they regarded themselves both as learners and, perhaps more crucially, from a humanitarian perspective, in terms of their inherent perceived value as worthy of love and happiness.

As I highlighted in the previous chapter, losing access to our capacity for creativity is like losing a part of our essence as humans. We're not meant to be creative to earn a second income or become a famous pop star, though that's an option for some, sure. We are *all* supposed to have the opportunity to engage with and enjoy creative practices and pursuits for the simple pleasure of doing them, regardless of our speculated aptitude for making them commercially viable pursuits.

My father introduced me to the arts, language, and travel, and both his parents had their own creative hobbies, which they shared with me. As a child, I didn't realise how lucky I was to have access to these things. At that age, I just assumed that everyone had the same experiences. As I got older, I lost contact with my creativity until it was just a distant memory. I remember being introduced once as an artist. I was a grown woman in a professional role and in that moment, I wanted the ground to open up and swallow me whole. I didn't feel like an artist, and I dreaded the question, "Oh wow, what do you do?" The term *creativity scars* is definitely one I can relate to, both throughout my school experience at the hands of teachers and through my peer group at the hands of immature, hormonal teens. I will be forever grateful to my father for defending my creativity when others sought to undermine and berate it.

Brené cautions that "Unused creativity is not benign – it turns into rage, shame and grief."

As we explored earlier, when we live without awareness, we often mistakenly link similar feelings together and assume we feel bad for one reason. More likely, it's a cocktail of experiences that we haven't spent time to decipher, each one feeding and fuelling the other.

So when I found myself in yet another period of life marked by flux, the unravelling of the familiar, and even more loss of control, I was so grateful to have begun the work of reclaiming myself as an artist, indulging in the Art of Being Human, in whatever form that would take.

Once again, I faced a choice between resisting the twists and turns of life as they came hurtling at me or accepting them and taking a step back to observe. The second option engenders much less suffering than the first, but neither can stop time from turning. One of life's few certainties is that change is inevitable; everything can, will and must change. This is a universal truth that I have brushed up against time and time again, but it took an intimate and devastating experience with grief for me to grasp the meaning of it fully. Learning to embrace this concept and perceive it from this vantage point has often freed me from mindlessly investing my energy into the panic of any given moment while allowing me to loosen my grip on the situation and trust in the absolute certainty of change.

The Buddhist principles of approaching suffering with mindfulness and compassion have underpinned how I navigated the turbulent waters of my encounter with grief, supported and nurtured, as you will see, with my creative practices to keep me anchored in a sense of humanity rather than despair.

Chapter Ten

Pre-Pregnancy

I want to share my journey into motherhood and the mysteries of nature beyond human understanding. The most significant milestones in a family's history are deaths and births. For my family, neither was anticipated. Both events will remain forever intertwined in my memory, the threads of one inextricably entangled with the other. This held true from the start, as even my discovery of one life was linked to losing another.

Before pregnancy, my life was consumed by an emotionally taxing job that continually tested my resilience despite my firm foundation. As mentioned, I was a youth and community worker serving marginalised populations facing multiple intersecting deprivations. Beyond the inherent psychological toll of addressing complex and competing needs, the organisational environments I worked in had grown dangerously toxic. Fear stifled communication, with words frequently taken out of context and misquoted for antagonistic effect. Deceit, hidden agendas, and revenge-driven motives were commonplace, leaving me feeling trapped in a relentless crossfire. I didn't need to convince myself that this space was unsafe; everything I saw and heard made it unmistakably clear.

I was operating well beyond full capacity when I received the most inconceivably tragic news. Someone that I love very dearly had lost her baby daughter, Hayley, on the day that we should have been celebrating her birth. I was at work when I got the call but had been planning to leave early to make my way to the hospital to welcome the new arrival into the world and our family. I'll never forget the shock of receiving the news. On one hand, it didn't feel real; at the same time, everything changed. It was the most heartbreaking thing I have ever witnessed, and I honestly felt the light in my world become dim from that moment.

For what felt like forever, I was unable to get past the cruelty and senselessness of it all. What had come to pass was incomprehensible to me. There had been no warning signs, no apparent cause for concern. Each one of us was utterly blindsided by the loss.

Hayley's one-year anniversary was a huge challenge for me. I didn't expect to feel so intensely emotional. At times, I felt like I didn't have the right to mourn her loss even half as hard as I did. This perception is quite common with the experience of vicarious trauma whereby you negate your right to feelings of grief, anguish and devastation because you weren't personally subjected to harm or injury. Therefore, you don't feel entitled to be as impacted as you are. And yet, when you watch someone you love go through something so unbearable, all the while feeling completely powerless to help or do anything, what else could you expect than to experience trauma vicariously?

All logic, reason, and practice of *Aparigraha* or non-grasping did not seem to stand up to the practical application I believed I had cultivated when I needed it most. I took the time to review how I had arrived at this point. I questioned everything I thought I knew, scrutinising previous interpretations of philosophies I'd presumed I had successfully integrated into my knowledge and experience. Indeed, we explore any of these universal truths not to acquire and accumulate knowledge but to apply and share that knowledge to minimise suffering and embody the qualities of these practices, even and especially when we feel least resourced to do so. Over time, this dedication typically results in a significant shift, impacting the quality of our day-to-day experiences, i.e. "that which we practise, grows." When our practices become habits, which become our culture, we can suddenly find that the practices have altered our physiological, psychological and spiritual states of Self. Through this commitment to continually return to a practice and baseline our experiences, we create the conditions for more substantial healing and transformation.

As I observed myself in this state of unknowing and uncertainty, I recognised that I didn't have command of my emotions and was struggling to function in my daily routine. I didn't believe myself to be particularly effective at handling any of my usual tasks, and yet, this time, it was a distinctly different feeling from when I had been here before. This is what I mean by baselining your experiences. I could recognise that I was not at all coping in the way I had so diligently cultivated, so I visited my doctor to report my concerns and to check in on what I thought was my deteriorating mental health. The doctor asked me if I could be pregnant, and I laughed. I really didn't take that question seriously, replying, "Not likely; I barely have an appetite for food at the minute!"

A few weeks later, I had an unusually tearful episode whilst at work, complete with terrifyingly dramatic heart palpitations. At thirty-three, I actually feared I could be having a heart attack brought on by a highly stressful work environment, equally challenging voluntary roles, and this most recent episode of profound grief. I stopped crying long enough to gather my things and left the office for home. Little did I know then that I would never return to that office again.

Twenty-four hours and three pregnancy tests later, it began to sink in that some of these symptoms were, in fact, due to my being pregnant and not, as I had convinced myself, a symptom of mental ill-health or a heart attack brought on by extreme stress. Upon learning this news, I was quickly faced with the choice, or as I prefer to see it, an entirely unreasonable social construct, of medicating myself with psychotropic drugs to return to a toxic work environment, versus leaving my profession to look after my health and in the process, likely kiss my career goodbye. The understanding that I was now entirely responsible for a life other than my own left me unable to reconcile the notion of risking continued, unnecessary strain on my body and sanity whilst asking my family to assume the burden of worrying about me and my unborn child for the next forty-plus weeks. The cost of remaining tied to money, security, and ego was now far too high for me to justify. I immediately resigned from almost all my occupations and vocational pursuits and began a new, pre-natal normal at home.

Chapter Eleven

Pregnancy

When I tell people that my pregnancy lasted ten months, it's not just a figurative nod to the wear and tear of gestation; my delivery occurred a fortnight after my forty-week due date, and I counted each one of those 294 days.

I very uncharacteristically spent the entirety of these forty-two weeks in a perpetual state of hormonally-induced tears. I cried for joy, sorrow, anxiety, anger, confusion, humour, and even boredom. Silly advertisements would catch me out, and I would become a blubbering heap. I couldn't hold myself together even if I tried.

If anyone who knew me had seen me while I was pregnant, they would be forgiven for thinking I'd lost the plot entirely and was having a mid-life crisis or a nervous breakdown. Coupled with my decision to withdraw from all of my social activities and professional titles, it must have appeared as though I had conceded defeat, given up under the weight of grief, conflict, and high-level stress, and laid down to wait for the storm to pass. But my body's symphony of thoughts, emotions, and sensations seemed to have an altogether different tone. While the above phrases are reasonable external interpretations and labels for what was happening, the description that resonates most with my internal existence at that time is finding serenity in surrender. Subconsciously embodying techniques that I had rehearsed during the Vipassana retreat, my pregnancy became an elongated exercise in mindfulness meditation.

For me now, meditation was an eyes-open practice. It meant that whatever position or activity I was in, I would move through it quietly and patiently, observing the present moment breath by breath, turning down all the extraneous noises so that I could view anything that arose internally with clarity and non-judgement. I wasn't a doer actively trying to design a way through this period in yang mode. I was passively waiting for an answer with receptive openness in yin mode. I was nestling completely into my femininity, and it was at utter odds with the masculinity of my typical day-to-day surroundings, much less the identity I had created for myself. This practice of embodying the sacred feminine was my most radical act to date, more than any other activist cause I have ever campaigned for.

Though not for the first time, I settled into a Stage Five feeling of *Groundedness*. Everything was in a state of flux; nothing felt familiar, much less stable. Yet, I trusted this transition and my capacity to navigate it, or at the very least, weather it with a degree of calm and relaxation. There was an interesting advantage to being so attuned to my own, at times barely recognisable rhythms. Occasionally, interspersed between the intervals of mindful watching, I experienced full-blown panic attacks: the complete package of total meltdown with hysterical wailing. Thankfully, since I had afforded myself the space to move slowly through each day, I was able to deduce that a single shot of caffeine from one cup of coffee was enough to tip me over the edge from being a regular crying mess to becoming an inconsolable, wailing banshee. As soon as I cut out the coffee, my panic attacks ceased.

The crying caused more awkwardness for others trying to adjust their understanding of my behaviour than it did for me. The only complaint I had was physical. I had developed an intense itchiness from the constant aggravation of my eyelids, which required eye drops to manage the enduring symptoms. I was curiously unbothered by my own crying as it was simply a physiological manifestation of my pregnancy without psychological significance. The witness of my meditative mind was able to sit back and note the crying as it was occurring, "Oh look, more tears," a biological happenstance, reacting to environmental conditions, like sweating or mouthwatering. The more I listened to myself intuitively, the more I could be honest with myself that some of the work and social settings outside of my home were not serving my welfare. If anything, they were inherently poisonous and unnecessarily dangerous.

Skinner was my absolute hero throughout the pregnancy, as with so many other times before. His unwavering support held zero expectations for me to do anything other than get through the day. He often came home from work to a wife still sporting last night's pyjamas, a kitchen stacked with dishes, or a pile of laundry lying untouched. I may have been sitting in the same place while he was at work, painting a mandala on my bump or endlessly strumming my ukulele. With the privilege of being unburdened by responsibility, I was able to withdraw and put up a protective bubble, studying sound therapy, teaching myself music on the ukulele, colouring in, immersing myself in nature, and revelling in any other creative pursuits that had been little more than unattainable luxuries when I'd been proverbially chained to a desk for work.

During my first trimester, after the awful morning sickness had subsided, I came across the song "Issues" by Julia Michaels and decided to learn it. Initially, I could not make it beyond the first verse without crying. I sensed that these were a new flavour of tears than I'd already experienced during the pregnancy. They were neither the omnipresent relaxed rivers streaming down the face nor were they the overstimulated shrieks of a panic attack. These were heartfelt, cathartic sobs that were releasing something. Perhaps it was my letting go of who I was before, breaking the ego, making way for the next variation of me.

If you're interested in learning more about the *Topography of Tears*, I highly recommend you look at Rose-Lynn Fisher's work. Seeing these images showed me just how meditators have described aspects of human anatomy, physiology and the experience of consciousness long before medical science could explain much of what they already knew to be true.

I spent an entire day learning that song and then recorded it to share on YouTube. Learning not to avoid this discomfort but rather to sit with it and move through it has become one of the universal practices that can be applied to any life experience and is a key factor in harnessing the potential of post-traumatic growth.

Engaging with music kept my mind active and soothed my nervous system. I felt more connected to the little human I was growing and was less caught up in worrying about the pregnancy. Given that the location where the ukulele is traditionally held over the belly is where my baby bump was, I could imagine that I was playing lullabies to my baby. This idea helped bolster my self-confidence around my maternal instincts. For the first time in my adult life, I was in service to no one other than myself, without guilt or concern for what others might think. Plenty of well-intentioned voices offered advice about how I could do pregnancy "better." I constantly had to refocus on following my instincts, reminding myself as much as anyone else that I knew what I needed, despite how it might have sometimes appeared.

I knew it looked like I was losing my mind. But I was always able to reassure myself that my conduct was rooted in mindfulness-based observations, critical thinking, and self-care. Regardless of what I may have, at times, felt compelled to do by the forces of peer pressure or social constructs, I was ultimately making the appropriate decisions for myself in the context of the information I had.

I should acknowledge that many people thoroughly enjoy their pregnancy and revel in the experience of becoming a parent, completely unhindered by any concerns or complications. I was not one of those people, and despite that, I want to stress that my experience resulted from a very specific set of circumstances and stressors. Now that I am out the other side of it, I am all the stronger for it. There is nothing that I can compare to the love you feel for your own child. It is, hands down, one of the most fulfilling things I have ever been privileged to be a part of.

Chapter Twelve

Birth

I gave birth to my son just after midday by emergency Caesarean section, having already spent two nights in the maternity hospital. I tried not to build up any expectations for how labour and delivery would go. It turned out to be as protracted and unsettled as the pregnancy, another mindfulness test and by no means a glamorous affair.

When I was two weeks beyond my due date, I had a "sweep" done at my local hospital, where they tried to agitate the cervix into active delivery. This was ineffective, and a few days later, I was brought in to the maternity hospital for induction and given a pessary, which is like a hormone-filled tampon (only more like a flat piece of string than a tube of cotton wool). I was then tethered up to machines and had a strap harnessed around my bump to monitor my blood pressure and the foetal heart rate. The pessary should have induced contractions within twenty-four hours if it was going to work at all, but twenty-four hours came and went uneventfully. Nothing! This "wain" wasn't for shiftin'!

I remember spending the night in the hospital on my own, determined that I was going to hold off on drugs until, and only if, I was in intolerable pain without them. I wasn't in a rush to take medication. I rarely do, even with migraines and menstrual cramps that have left me lying on the floor for days at a time. I generally opt for letting symptoms run their course whenever possible. I have often found hydration and good nutrition, coupled with rest, to be the most effective plan of action, likely because of treating the issue rather than the symptom.

On top of this, though, I'd been holding onto a limiting moralistic belief that I hadn't realised I'd been harbouring about wanting a natural birth, like a "proper yoga teacher," because apparently in my skewed mental universe, women yogis somehow were in complete command of their labour journeys! Sure enough, almighty Mother Nature showed her hand in her own time, unearthing this delusion and setting me straight. Oh, how my perspective on this whole experience has shifted over the years, informed by overlapping strands of the different parts of my experiences. If I were to do labour again now, I expect things would look and feel very different, but of course, with this, as with all things, there are no guarantees, and it's easy to say such things in hindsight.

My contractions finally started in the wee hours of the morning, and I phoned Skinner in agony at 6 am, asking him to come back to the hospital as soon as possible because I needed him by my side. I was scared, not that I could admit that to myself then, and I didn't want to be alone. By the time he arrived, I was doubled over on the side of the bed. I couldn't stand up, and I couldn't sit down. Even then, I remained hesitant to accept pain relief, only caving when a nurse reminded me that the hormones from the pessary had artificially forced my body into an endeavour that it didn't have time to catch up with. That was all the rational information I needed, or perhaps for the first time, it was delivered so that I could hear it. Not long after that intervention, I was totally wiped out on painkillers, "away with the fairies," as we say here. I was hungry for hash browns, practically licking my own eyebrows and putting my Mum and sisters in kinks of laughter with my slurred speech and nonsensical murmurings.

Labour was long. Numerous women had come and gone from our shared ward. Then, after forty hours of contractions, the staff wheeled me into a private side room. It was my turn! The nurse produced what appeared to be a metre stick with a pointy hook on the end of it to break my waters. My husband turned green, then grey and started sweating at the sight of the instrument. It took two attempts to do the deed, and after the first one, Skinner looked like he might pass out, so I sent him away for a cup of coffee and some fresh air. He's never been great with needles, so this must have been some next-level gore to see up close and personal. The doctor put me on a cortisol drip to continue to push my body into labour, doubling the dose at intervals to increase the contractions. After some coaxing from the nurse, I acquiesced to undergoing an epidural injection in my spine, a diamorphine drip, plus gas and air. The staff used an ice cube to test the level of anaesthesia, and on the right side of my body, I could still feel everything from just above the knee all the way up past my belly button. The anaesthetic should have kicked in and taken all sensation away from there by now, so I shouldn't have been able to feel anything. I remained in this limbo state of a half-numb body for five hours because the anaesthetist had to leave partway through to attend to a couple of other emergency deliveries elsewhere in the hospital.

I committed to keeping calm while waiting for the anaesthetist to return, reminding myself that I was fortunate not to need emergency intervention like their other patients. “God love those women,” I kept thinking, which is exactly what my mother would say while breaking her heart over being unable to do more for them. I’ve always been in awe of my mother's capacity for empathy. Her care is boundless. At times, I have wondered if it was to her detriment as I felt it cost her so much of herself, but at other times, it has taught me about compassion. When we tend towards extremes in these experiences, it’s rarely good for us, but if we can find balance in the midst of it all, then we can cultivate a human kindness that the world could do with more of, especially at this point in time. Learning not to look away from other people’s pain while not being consumed by it, is a lifetime practice and one that I didn’t fully appreciate the nuances of until I was much older. The potential for healing when someone is witnessed in all of their pain without fear of judgement, shouldn’t be underestimated.

After the second attempt at the epidural failed, I was done with the expectation of being pain-free. I was not afraid to endure temporary physical discomfort. I could console myself that I at least still felt safe. That was all I needed to know. I can't remember many thought processes during this stage. I was very detached from my body and had mentally handed myself over to the professionals. I kick myself now for not using any of the hypnobirthing techniques I had learned, but I equally feel like there could've been some cues, support or encouragement to try those things, which weren't available when I needed them.

The elements I remember remain indelible in my mind years later and are surprisingly trivial. I don't remember the nurses' names, for example, even though I remember telling one that I would name my baby after her as I was being wheeled out of the room. I have a vivid recall of the squeaks of their markers as they charted my son's arrival on the whiteboard with medical jargon and the feeling of relief when the fluorescent lights went out on the ward at the end of the day that allowed me to feel less exposed, and at the same time uncovered the sight of streetlights and neon chip shop signs out through the huge windows overlooking Belfast's Newtownards Road.

I drifted in and out of sleep halfway through the night. Every time I lay on my left side, the baby's heart rate dropped, so I would be woken by the nurse now and again and told to turn onto my other side. A tough few hours of worried dozing passed. When morning arrived, and the next obstetrician took up his shift in the ward, I was informed by proxy that I was about 9 cm dilated. The doctor turned to an intern and said, "You can see the hair there, can't you?" They were so casually discussing me and my situation, without even acknowledging me, that I cheekily asked if there was anyone else they'd like to invite in for a look. I wish I had understood the cue of how dilated I was at that point to even try to visualise what my body needed to do next.

Instead, a surgeon came in to consult on the possibility of a Caesarean section. I could barely talk at this point, and my monkey mind was getting carried away with all kinds of questions, a heady cocktail of anxiety and frustration, questioning the staff's lack of urgency. I was afraid, yet still feeling so grateful for having hope. The vast reserve of gratitude I could access more than balanced the intermittent spikes of fear as they arose. Despite that, I wasn't up for taking any risks. The whole way through my pregnancy, I hadn't dared allow myself to believe that I would get to take my baby home from the hospital. That was all I was hoping for, and until it happened, there were no guarantees. Minutes after consenting to surgery, I was wheeled into the operating theatre.

I feel like I had never been informed of, nor prepared for, the intensity of a C-section. I was handled like a slab of meat being tossed around on a butcher's block. I was sitting on a gurney, heaped over myself, being propped up and contorted into different angles and poses to allow the long epidural needle to be inserted in a straight line along my spinal column. I could hear the delivery team sympathetically postulate over my shoulder, "Awk, God love her," "Awk, she must be exhausted," "Awk, poor wee woman." Though well-intentioned, their cooing didn't soothe me. It made me realise how weak and vulnerable I truly felt. I'd become apathetic by now, wishing someone would knock me out and wake me up when there was some good news.

They put a blue screen up, hovering just above my chest and stopped shy of my face. I didn't feel anything for a time. I saw Skinner enter the operating theatre in blue scrubs, and then he came and stood by my shoulder. I felt an enormous pressure unlike anything else I've ever felt before. I worried that something had gone horribly wrong because I felt this tonne-weight descend on my chest. Struggling to breathe, I thought, "Fuck, did my lungs just collapse there? What's going on?" Turns out that's actually the medic putting pressure on the top of the womb to push the baby out, almost like squeezing out a tube of toothpaste. How unexpected to feel so inanimate at the point of bringing new life into the world.

When my son was born, he didn't cry. I will never forget that sound of silence. They took him over to a table at the side of the room, and Skinner ran back and forth like a man possessed, telling me, "Ten fingers, ten toes! He's got a nose and two ears." I recall turning to him and saying in a barely audible whisper, "I really need to try and pull myself together here now, so I need you to be in charge for the next wee while, okay?" I was lying on the stone-cold table, trying to tell the nurses that I was so cold, practically convulsing with it. They told me they would get me sorted out soon. They had the baby wrapped in cloth, and they set him on my neck and face. I couldn't quite locate my hands; I felt like I was going to drop him. As for the proud father, he embraced us both, taking selfies and grinning from ear to ear. Seeing the photos of this now always makes me think of the statues holding baguettes at the Dalí Museum in Barcelona! It's just so odd. This little baby baguette set across my collarbone.

They took my husband and son to another room together while they finished stitching me back up. When that surgical procedure was complete, they took me to my boys and helped me sit up to do skin-to-skin for the first time. That is another feeling I will remember for the rest of my life.

From start to finish, the surgical procedure took about forty minutes. I still feel its impact on my body years later.

Chapter Thirteen

Leaving the Hospital

I usually feel blessed to have a home in the countryside where nature is always on my doorstep. Still, the surreal drive home from the hospital along our pothole-speckled back roads became a jolting lesson on one of the downsides of rural living as we bounced along in what felt like the roughest yet slowest-moving vehicle I'd ever been in. I winced with every bump and grimaced with every ditch our car traversed, excruciatingly aware of the surgical stitches tentatively holding my entire abdomen together, preventing my organs from spilling out all over the floor. I don't think I've ever been so glad to see our driveway come into view as I was that day.

Arriving home, achingly tired after days in the hospital with little sleep, and realising that we had nothing but a Moses basket and blanket in the house was overwhelming. A combination of relief and the sudden immensity of what was unfolding before us started to sink in as we crossed the threshold. The next day, the midwife came to visit. She checked the baby's latch, among other things, to ensure we were getting to grips with feeding. She was happy with how I was getting on, but then, surprisingly, a few days later, I hit my limit.

It's a pretty graphic story about why I stopped breastfeeding, so brace yourself, or if that's not your cup of tea, feel free to skip ahead to the next chapter.

I breastfed for maybe the next five or so days, but it got more and more agonising, excruciating even. At this point, I kept going, you know. I just kept trying, telling myself, “You can do this.” It must have been around St Patrick's Day, that’s the 17th of March if you’re reading this and you’re not Irish! I was at home on my own, feeding the baby. Skinner had gone shopping for groceries, probably to get some compresses for my nipples, which felt like they were covered in paper cuts! My son was still very much a newborn, barely a week old. He was feeding with his eyes closed; you could hold all of him with one arm. There he was, latched on and feeding well, and the next thing I knew, he just stopped and spat out. I looked down, and crimson-red blood was all over my light, pastel-coloured bedclothes. It was like something straight out of a horror movie! I was home alone, just me and him, and I shit a brick!

I can't remember in detail what I did next, but I know I sat him upright and put my finger inside his mouth to check where the blood had come from. My finger came out totally clean. No blood. Something didn’t make sense. I took some clean tissue and checked again. Nothing. I did the same with a white muslin cloth. No blood anywhere. At that point, I thought maybe I was so sleep-deprived that I was making it up. I couldn't understand where the blood came from, but the proof was on the now blood-stained bedclothes. So I phoned the midwife and texted Skinner. By the time he arrived home, I was like, “That’s it! I'm done with breastfeeding. That was terrifying!” Honestly, for me, it was one of the most visually traumatising things imaginable. What was most alarming was the colour and amount of blood. It wasn't a gob of saliva with a speck of blood; it was pure red, opaque liquid, and it seemed like an awful lot proportionally to have come out of such a tiny person.

The midwife told me on the phone that this was pretty standard, and she didn't need me to bring my son in to get checked out. Pretty standard? How so, now? Apparently, it's quite a common occurrence in breastfeeding; if the latch is shallow, even if it's almost perfect, breastfeeding mothers will be very prone to getting tiny slices in the nipples, which can't be seen with the naked eye. So I couldn't have known they were there, apart from the near-blinding pain, that is. Also, it wouldn't be unheard of for babies to take a mouthful of blood and then spit it out so that they can get at the milk ducts. Part of me thought, "Is it any wonder they don't tell you that? It would put you right off." But part of me also thought, "Seriously, a little heads-up would have been great!" So, hubby was sent out to the shops again, this time for a box of formula and some bottles. And that was the end of breastfeeding for about two weeks.

I had many low days during this time, now that I think of it. That's pretty standard for new mothers as our bodies work to rebalance hormones after hosting a human, or foreign body as it can also be described, for the best part of a year. There was a lot of crying from the baby and me! I remember thinking, "I'm so tired... maybe I can't do this," but I was so delirious in the newborn phase or fourth trimester that I didn't know what was happening, especially as this was my first child. I remember it being tough and exhausting. I felt entirely useless.

Around this time, I was finishing my Clexane injections, which are to prevent blood clots after surgery. For six days, I had to self-administer injections into my leg. Pre-pregnancy, I was covered in body piercings. I removed a lot of them during my pregnancy. I have never been scared of needles and am usually comfortable enough and curious enough to watch as I'm being injected or pierced. But now, after a C-section, the thoughts of this needle, and it was really just a teeny, tiny, insignificant prick, was just too intrusive; I could feel that my body didn't want it. I had been through enough. It took me a long time to realise that my intense aversion to these needles was an indication of just how low my physical and mental resilience had become, just how traumatised I felt from the whole experience of labour. I was all out of spoons, and the last thing I needed was to be faced with any more challenges.

Back to breastfeeding. I think my body needed the break after the whole induced labour and emergency C-section episode. So when I decided I was going to stop breastfeeding, the next thing was figuring out how to actually stop! I searched online; people said to take mint and/or use cabbage leaves! I remember thinking, "Is this for real?" I knew I had some food-grade peppermint essential oil at home, and I drank shots of that mixed with water while walking around with cabbage leaves stuffed in my bra! I dread to think what I looked or smelled like, but it worked, or so I thought. I woke up one morning, and one breast had gone down considerably, but the other breast was so engorged it was solid, like a wrecking ball! It was bigger than my actual head, I swear! It was bizarre looking in the extreme. So there I was walking around with one EE-size boob, and then this, I don't know, XXXL boob, thinking, “What the fuck am I meant to do with this? Throw it over my shoulder? How am I supposed to live my life like this?” This continued for maybe three or four days. A week even, who knows? People were calling to visit and see the baby and, when I was holding the baby in front of me, they would put their arm underneath to lift him, and all I could think was, “Oh my God, please don't notice my massive wrecking ball boob!”

I was trying to disguise the wonky boob situation under my baggy clothes, and if anyone had told me that might be one of the side effects, I would have just thought, “No thanks. I'm not playing!” but you just don't know what to expect. My mindset changed back and forth that whole time too, because part of me was thinking, “It's really impressive what the human body can do,” while another part was thinking, “Why? How? There's nothing reasonable about what is happening to my body right now.” I will never get that image out of my head of just one ginormous wrecking-ball boob. So there were definitely funny moments, and there were moments when I found myself thinking, “If I don't laugh, I'll cry,” and for as many of those I had, there were just as many moments of, “Actually fuck it, I am just going to cry.”

I decided to breastfeed again, through guilt, I think, or at least that’s the closest word I have to describe it, but I hadn’t felt guilt quite like this before. It’s hard to explain. It wasn't like I felt any pressure from my family or anything. When I was pregnant and going to all the antenatal appointments, I would rebel against the advice, assumptions and expectations quite a lot. I was trying hard to manage my expectations, so at every appointment, when they asked me if I was going to breastfeed, I would say, “We'll see.” It was never like, “This is my goal, and it's all I'm hoping for.” It’s not like I went back to breastfeeding under duress, but it wasn't a logical process, either. I didn’t have negative feelings of “I must try harder.” It was a much more subtle, positive sense of relief and resilience, almost like I felt my body and mind had rallied from the relative rest, and we agreed that we could venture one more mammoth effort for this very temporary set of circumstances.

I spoke with Skinner about it, and then we went together to see the midwife in the hospital, and she was a tonic. She said it was entirely up to me. “That wee child is thriving and is quite happy with a bottle,” she said. I was barely holding it together at this point, but her kindness opened the floodgates, and I dissolved into tears. Then she told me that it's not unheard of for mothers to re-lactate. “If this is really something you want to do, we're all here to support you, but that child is happy, so you do what you want to do, not what you think you should do.” She was brilliant. I was lucky to have a midwife like Ashlene in the Downe Hospital. She made a world of difference to my experience. She made me feel capable, strong and worthy when I was feeling my absolute worst, and I hope she knows how incredible she is at her job.

So, I made a second attempt at breastfeeding, and it didn’t feel anything like the life-or-death situation I’d experienced a few short weeks before. Compared to the first week after he was born, when everything felt intense, this time, it was more like, “Well, even if he gets one ounce of breastmilk a day, then that’s a success.” It was the complete opposite experience the second time, which helped. It took all the pressure off me. When babies are still so young, they build your milk supply as they grow, and they grow really fast in those first few months, so in reality, we didn’t have that much ground to make up.

The lactation process was beautiful to witness and participate in without the same urgency or fears as my first experience. I especially liked seeing how quickly the body can accommodate meeting another person's needs. We’re talking about going from producing a few droplets of milk in a twenty-minute session of pumping and expressing to producing eight to ten ounces in five minutes just from one breast while simultaneously feeding a similar amount from the other! Making this leap in a matter of weeks opened my eyes to how quickly our bodies can adapt significantly when the demands we put on it change, and at times, if I’m honest, I felt like I was dreaming it. Don't get me wrong, I had plenty of tough days too. It wasn’t all magical awe and wonder. I ended up with milk blisters on my already traumatised nipples, which were now also experiencing Raynaud's Syndrome. I had mastitis infection in the milk ducts and all that other fun stuff that you don’t know about until you do. But the stronger and more capable I felt with each passing day, the less any of that superficial, temporary stuff mattered. It all paled into insignificance.

Breastfeeding had other physical impacts on my body and one day, I realised I had a lot of pain and tension in my neck and upper back. I noticed I was feeding more from one side than the other, which scrunched me up on one side. So, I decidedly started to bring my awareness back into my body, observing my posture during breastfeeding and preparing where I would sit before feeding sessions to have plenty of props, cushions and support. That really simple intervention saved me a world of pain in the long run. I found that I was still very much cowering as though I was in pain while feeding, even though the pain no longer existed. It was like an emotional hangover from a physical experience, and it took me to consciously train that habit out, much like you need to train out a limp after you've recovered from an injured foot. Undoubtedly, my background in yoga and meditation helped me nip unwanted habits in the bud early, but anyone can do these things. You don't need a formal yoga or meditation practice; you simply need to develop your awareness.

A few months into becoming a mum, I noticed it was Maternal Mental Health Week, so I made a full week of videos for my social media page. One of the videos was a yoga session specifically for the neck and shoulders for breastfeeding mothers, inspired by what I noticed in my body. The information that mothers are given about breastfeeding is very scattered. I have a friend who has four kids, and she didn't realise until her last one that she could continue to breastfeed beyond six months. She thought that was the ultimate goal - six months, and you're done. Like, you're not allowed to go over those six months! She was told that wasn't the case with her last baby and continued feeding her youngest until around three years old. So I don't think there's any consistency with the messaging. It seems very much down to the personal perspective of whoever's conveying the message. And actually, sadly, we see that across broader healthcare policy in Northern Ireland as standard. It's a postcode lottery no matter your condition, it would seem, subject to whoever is appointed as your healthcare provider and their own personal opinion on the matter.

Before I became a mother, I would have been one of those people who said, "If they've a head full of teeth and they can eat and drink normal food, then they don't need breastmilk anymore," which shows how our culture here is attitudinally towards things like breastfeeding because what is breast milk apart from the most natural thing in the world!

I fed my son until he was two and a half years old. It's one of those things where everyone's experience is so unique and, at times, traumatic that the last thing anybody needs is extra external judgement. Whether you find it easy and natural or difficult and elusive, it's one of the biggest things you'll ever do or never do with your body, and it stays with you far beyond the nursing stages of parenting.

I was never approached disapprovingly while feeding in public, and I would like to have seen anyone try that with me. Yet, I still found that I developed a degree of shame in general about how my body was functioning, especially regarding breastfeeding. That was difficult at times. I even felt ashamed about combination feeding, where you start each feed on the breast to stimulate milk production, then follow up with formula. Over time, you can begin to drop formula feeds as they are getting enough from the breast. Imagine that. I felt ashamed for trying to ensure my son's health. How insane is that? I managed to feed my son, relactate and increase my milk supply to the point where I was able to feed him exclusively on breastmilk from two to six months, had a plentiful freezer stash for us as needed so that other family members could also do feeds, and I donated four litres of milk to the Human Milk Bank which is used to support premature babies. Imagine feeling ashamed of that.

I think part of the self-deprecating here links back to being a yoga teacher who didn't have a natural birth and then failed at the only other thing my body is built specifically to do. I felt deeply ashamed that my body had let me down, and I had never felt so lonely. I love to be alone, as I've said but experiencing loneliness is a completely different thing. This opened my eyes to the experience of living with enduring conditions. So filled with frustration and desperation.

I had only just decided to move away from my professional career to prioritise this pregnancy and get back into my yoga and meditation. Still, I experienced feelings of inadequacy, creating another trap of burdens and expectations I was trying to live up to. Pressure is everywhere; we must be vigilant when we're not in the driving seat and being driven remotely instead. Learning that I don't have to opt into others' expectations has been one of my biggest lessons. If you notice those thoughts in yourself, those burdensome, heavy and unwelcome sensations, one of the easiest ways out is through movement. Learning to move your body, whether through structured, regimented practices or improvised, playful exploration, helps to filter out the noise of external influences and negative self-talk from your mind.

As always, the more you practise, the easier it becomes.

Chapter Fourteen
Freedoms

I decided to leave my job and cut out everything else, choosing instead to stay somewhere where I could prioritise safety for me and the bump as much as possible. In doing so, I sacrificed many of my personal freedoms, or rather, put them on hold.

When I got home from the hospital with my son, I realised there was no peer support group or mums and tots meet-ups in our area. I couldn't afford to travel to Belfast every day to see friends. I didn't want to have people over to visit either; it was just too much to concern myself with. I was worried about what people would think about combination feeding: "Why are you going to breastfeed if you're just going to follow it up straight after with a bottle of formula?" I couldn't face the idea of continually having to repeat myself, my choices and the rationale for them. So, isolation seemed like the easiest option. It offered a level of assurance to mitigate unnecessary incoming stressors, and it also took the pressure off trying to leave the house.

Honestly, I rarely get out the door on time when I've just got myself to organise. Trying to get out of the house with a newborn and hoping you've remembered all the things you might need, lest you face a nappy explosion in the middle of the supermarket and have to take your baby home in a smelly old hoodie that was in the back of the car because you forgot to pack a clean change of clothes since the last time you dared to venture out, doesn't really feel like a constructive use of time and definitely doesn't make you feel like you're about to win any "Mother-of-the-Year" awards. This is particularly true when your sleep is rationed, your hormones are all over the place, and you're doing most of the day-to-day stuff alone because your partner had to go back to work soon after the birth.

I felt I had many reasons to limit myself in what I was doing, even though I know my friends would've been incredibly understanding and supportive. I could count on one hand how many of them made it over my threshold in those few weeks, and I was so grateful to them for making me feel so at ease. Then, a girl called Catherine reached out to me. She is one day younger than me, a community worker like me, and she lives about the same distance from me to the nearest town, but on the other side of the town. Her wee one was born about six weeks after mine, the same thing, two weeks overdue, emergency C-section. Due to her location, she couldn't access the post-natal community support she needed either, so she, I and another girl called Roisin started up our own Mothers' Group. It was very casual initially, just tea and sympathy at each other's houses. It quickly turned into a voluntary group, open to anyone.

Catherine and Roisin were great at reaching out to other mums through the breastfeeding group in town, which was open to everyone. The culture they created meant that other mums felt safe to do the same. So the group grew to about thirty mums at one stage. We had regular weekly meet-ups, and any time people were free outside of that, mums could post in the WhatsApp chat to see if anyone else was available. We were, and are now still, some years later, called the Monday Mummies. Catherine has undoubtedly been the glue that has held us all together, and all credit to her for being that constant when so many of us were transitioning to and from other things.

So, stuff like that was really helpful in those weird days of social isolation as a new mum, before social isolation was an almost indiscriminate global experience as we saw with the pandemic. I'm not the kind of person who seeks out support groups, but I've turned to this network many times, just looking for reassurance and connection. I now consider many of those mums to be close friends. At the inception of this group, I saw it as an opportunity to support a friend. I had no idea we would end up forging a community of sisterhood with bonds that would last a lifetime. These women are my village. I will be eternally indebted to them for their support, and I ache at the thought of other women having to go through these experiences alone.

When you have your first child, it feels like you are changing gears. I was talking to a friend the other day, and she was describing her experience of navigating chronic illness. She said it was like I described having kids in the sense that your old friends keep waiting for you to return to normal so you can go out and play again. I thought, "Yeah, that's pretty spot on, isn't it?" It's the same experience. Isolation. Grief. Something we all understand a lot better since the global pandemic. So, that's probably where I noticed my lack of freedom the most. Pre-baby, it would've been pretty normal for me to go out to work in the morning and then go and stay with a friend in the city in the evening. Whether participating in an open mic or going to samba practice, I would have a few drinks with friends and drive home at lunchtime the following day. As a youth worker, my schedule was always a bit abstract, facilitating my social life during the week. When I found out I was pregnant, that all came to a halt.

I do enjoy my own company, and I've done a lot of work to get to a place where I can say that sincerely, but I can't say I've dealt with not having those freedoms because there's still a part of me that thinks someday I'll catch up with my friends again too. I didn't go back to anything from my old life or any of my hobbies or voluntary roles in the first few years after becoming a parent. I felt if I was going to make space for this new person in our lives in a meaningful way, I would have to do that, not just seeing where they could fit into an existing situation, but creating that space for them and building our life around them. That was the perspective I brought to how I would make these decisions. It was very much like, “Well, I'm not going through this several times, so this kid is pretty special!”

I had an unexpected shift of perspective around that time, and I started to see everyone I met as a holy miracle, you know, once you realise how precious life is. It was also a wonder to me how so many of us even make it to the age of becoming parents because the early days of raising a child are just so peppered with difficult and scary moments. So, in terms of choosing not to see my friends, I can’t say it felt like a choice. They weren't decisions I made; they were just priorities. I'm pragmatic enough to recognise that I can meet only so many priorities at any one time. I suppose retrospectively, you can see how isolated you are, but at the time, you're so busy with a newborn that you really are just getting on with it. Weeks and months pass in the blink of an eye. So there was me and everything I went through as one priority, and then there was my son as an autonomous part of that whilst being a full-time dependent. Then there was everything else that I had beyond our family unit of three, which all just kind of blurred into the background for a while.

When I was pregnant, I grieved for the life that I had lost; I grieved for the fact that I had invested myself entirely into a career that I didn't want anymore. Despite the circumstances which brought me to this place, the more I talk to friends and loved ones, the more I realise that many of us go through this stage of adult development around this time in our lives. It's not categorically related to becoming a parent, so much as it's leaving the young adult threshold and moving onto a more mature persona.

I grieved for not being able to go out with friends. I love my friends. They're some of the most incredible people I've ever had the fortune to meet. I had a very relaxed lifestyle before my pregnancy and was really happy with it. I loved how I travelled, the company I kept, and the opportunities I had been able to take on a whim. And truth be told, it wouldn't be long until I could take up my travels and pursue my interests once more.

It should come as no surprise then that one of the first things we did when we got my son's name on a birth certificate was to get him a passport. That was a non-negotiable priority, setting the tone for his future. I was determined we would travel while he was little, and he would know what that was like growing up. The rest was just a basic understanding that this transition had occurred, acknowledging that things would never be the same again and that any illusion of control at this point was long gone.

In his first year of life, we went to festivals. Of course, it wasn't the same. I'm not saying we wouldn't do it again; we did many times, but it's a completely different experience. We went to one of the festivals when he was just two months old. We took him on a plane to the Grand Northern Ukulele Festival in Huddersfield - "GNUF." It was my first time performing solo at a ukulele festival, and it was his first time travelling on a plane and a train and attending a festival, apart from the previous year when he was in utero! These things gave me more hope, something to aim for, and an excuse to prioritise creativity and myself postpartum. Why do we feel like we need to justify allocating time for creativity?

Working towards festival appearances wasn't about regaining ground that I had lost temporarily to facilitate this new person's arrival. It was very much like every birth is an opportunity for everybody to come out of it a different person, so I intentionally considered what that might look like for me. I never sat down with a list to make strategic decisions about the direction I wanted to go in, but I did spend time meditating on the things that made me happy, relaxed, and feel connected to people outside my family unit. I prioritised those things as critical to my well-being and worthy of my attention, knowing that these things would inevitably enhance who and how I was at home.

Chapter Fifteen

Early Motherhood

In early motherhood, I spent a lot of time reflecting on the valuable things I had learned through all my well-being practices. I wanted to keep doing things that made me uncomfortable, but I had to balance the level of challenge and stress I was absorbing so that it didn't push me over the edge in my new normal of sustaining a dependent. I wasn't frantically trying to get somewhere, but I had a very measured determination to keep going, rest when I needed to, and know that another opportunity was on the horizon. The best of me definitely wasn't behind me.

The funny thing about having a kid is that your understanding of language and specific words changes significantly. Other people talk about their kids, and if you don't have kids, you can't grasp any of that because it's far beyond your frame of reference. If you have children, it almost feels like you become part of the world's best-kept secret. When you see other parents, and they tell you they're knackered, you suddenly get it, you totally understand. Those words greet you with an entirely new force. "I feel the weight of what you've just said. I've been there and lived it, and I get it." You relate to other people in a completely different way, and you've not had the language for maybe thirty years of your life. Oddly, the words are still exactly the same. When I say language, I mean the intention behind the communicated words. The felt sense of the words. That was one of the really interesting things I experienced:

suddenly developing new connections and bonds, some with total strangers, through shared experiences of common feelings.

Likewise, throughout my meditation journey, I just assumed it was the same experience for everyone. Yet, when this tiny teacher arrived in my life, my understanding of consciousness significantly shifted once more. When I was pregnant, I described a sense of feeling like a lodger in my own body. It was like I lived there and knew the place like home but was very aware that I was also sharing the space with a roommate, one who consistently outgrew their side of the room and further encroached onto mine. But then, when he had finally left his haven and arrived into the world as a separate entity, an aspect of my consciousness seemed to go with him. It was almost as though my consciousness, while still tethered to me, was solely concerned with the safety of our latest addition. So, I could be in a conversation with someone and not hear a single word they said because my awareness was overseeing a play session on the other side of the room. You might recognise this when you try to speak to a mother over the top of the sound of her baby crying. You will likely observe that the mother can't hear you. Yes, her musculoskeletal system is there right in front of you, but her conscious awareness that you seek to communicate with is otherwise engaged and quite literally *unable to come to the phone right now*.

When I think of some of my female friends who started having children in their twenties, I have such massive respect for them, especially those who have more than one child! You know? "Absolute heroines! I applaud you all. That's a *lot* of work." The same goes for single parents and people with twins and triplets. I can't fathom how they do it. How do they get dressed? How do they have time to wash? I look at my mum who, has five children, and I think, "You are some woman; that is incredible!" I mean, some of the stories that she could tell you would make your eyes water! If you don't already know the story of how you came into this world, and you have the luxury of being able to ask your parents, I encourage you to have that conversation. Meet your parents on a human level and listen to their stories of transition and transformation.

For now, though, I'll return to some of the concepts I mentioned and finish some thoughts on this whole-life overhaul. Something worth remembering in all of this, even when you learn these life lessons about impermanence, is that it doesn't mean you're finished understanding them. As I described earlier, it's about learning to balance; you learn it, yes, but you must keep working at it to maintain it. It's important to develop it as a culture or habit, not simply understand notionally what it is. It's very easy to be afraid of feeling like you're out of control. When you feel like this, you may resent yourself and end up in a spiral of doubt and self-depreciation. It feels counterintuitive, but you can find the most peace by learning to relinquish control, to freefall, suspended in the unknown. The illusion of control causes unnecessary and often invisible suffering.

When you hit a low point, don't allow negative self-talk to run rampant in your head and exacerbate those feelings. Instead, acknowledge the inevitability that in life, like with the very breath itself, you will experience rise and fall. You can't have highs without lows. It's not the ebb and flow of life that causes suffering. It's the meanings that we attach to each cycle of oscillation that make it all so uncomfortable. Practise learning to exhale as you let go and learn to view each breath as a rebirth.

When you become a parent, it can sometimes feel like everyone has something important to say. And I'm wary of advising in black and white because everyone's experience differs. It's a full spectrum. But for me, I have to say that, having never gone through any of this before, I had to keep reminding myself, "You can't know what you don't know." All too often, when we breach the construct of our former selves, we berate ourselves about the outcome of a scenario, forgetting that we have since gained the added benefit of hindsight. We must be more gracious with ourselves, viewing failure as a fundamental milestone and an essential element in any change and learning process. In some cultures and pursuits, like weightlifting, failure is central to building success. The term "repeat till failure" is a way to ensure progression. There is nothing to fear in failure. If we fear failure, we must look behind the word to understand the why.

When I think about my birthing experience in the context of the decisions I had to make regarding medical interventions, a positive outcome for me far outweighed any autonomy I might have hoped to have over clinical decisions. Knowing there was a risk I might not get to take my baby home at all, I'd have signed up for anything.

That being said, a C-section is major abdominal surgery, and I never really appreciated that before personally experiencing it. Things would be very different if I ever did it a second time, and yet, I know full well that I would be at the mercy of whatever would unfold. I would trust my body more with the knowledge I've gained. It's incredible how we come to be in this world. Yet, throughout our lives, we learn to disrespect and diminish ourselves in all manner of ways to fit in. To remain safe within the pack. Tragic really.

I regard a lot of how I understand my experience as a series of trauma responses. I suppose that's what put me off making decisions and engaging in external processes during pregnancy - I didn't do a birth plan, for example. I didn't want to set myself up for expectations that I couldn't meet. I found it was much easier to manage my expectations if they were very low. And that was pretty much focusing on the now. Getting through each breath. I didn't have an outfit for leaving the hospital, for example. I get that's a superficial example, yet, culturally, it was something I'd heard people talk about quite a bit when I was pregnant. I couldn't picture it, even though I'm a very visual person. I was totally in denial, which is a natural psychological and neurological response activated to keep me safe. But parts of my conduct that may have looked like collapse or fawn response from the outside were intentional and deliberate decisions to withdraw, to retreat and shelter and, as I learned on the retreat, just as I learned from my first attempt at breastfeeding, were essential for creating the conditions for me to rest, then return renewed.

The only advice I could give to anyone in a similar position is that *you* have to live with your decisions; not the doctor, the midwife, or your well-meaning family or friend at the end of the phone - just you. So, listen to yourself first. If you can't hear your own thoughts for the noise of others, begin a journaling practice. Put pen to paper without expectation, and just see what comes out. You might be surprised to discover how you really feel.

One of the biggest challenges I faced over the last few years was letting go of the identity I had spent fifteen years curating. There was no way I could live up to the expectation of who she was, and there was no way I wanted to! That was definitely an episode of grief on its own. Still, somewhere in these periods of transition, I could ease into discomfort, relax into knowing that this was only ever going to be temporary and understand that I would come out the other side of it eventually. I'm avoiding referring to an *improved version of myself* because I don't want people to feel that they always need to be improved or improving to be valued. Still, I knew with absolute clarity that parts of transition are ripe with opportunity if you don't pour all of your energy into reeling against them. It's like hitting a wave head-on or steering into a skid. Sometimes, the right course of action appears counterintuitive, but it's the only thing that works. You learn that it's not even about bracing yourself for impact. It's trusting that the effect is nothing. If you're relaxed enough, everything else is irrelevant, inconsequential and transient.

I recognise that I was very privileged in that I could choose to stay home without having to work while pregnant, but I also think it comes down to priorities and perspectives. I sacrificed a lot to create that bubble. I'm not saying everyone can; of course not. But so often, we don't feel like we can take the time to consider our options. It's almost as if we believe the decisions are already out of our hands. I challenge you to test this in your own life. You'd be surprised where you end up when you make decisions more consciously. If you have enough respect for yourself to be kind - I mean diligently, compassionate, and radically accepting of yourself, you'll make some decisions you didn't expect. Loosen your grip, go with the flow, and enjoy the scenery.

One of the key things I learned during my Vipassana meditation retreat is that I don't need to learn things the hard way. Whenever I felt like I was punishing myself or pushing too hard, I would spend longer on that decision and unpack it. "Is this my internal monologue, or is this somebody else's expectation talking through my thoughts?" When you learn to decipher these subtle distinctions, it doesn't matter what the material aspects of your decisions are; it's just about ensuring you can return to your values and ethics as the basis for your decisions.

In the work that I have done and in all my interactions, I engage through the lens of trauma. That resulted from growing up in Northern Ireland and my vocational studies that supported my chosen career, which is my frame of reference. I assume almost everyone is acting from a place of complex and intersecting trauma responses. That's not an unreasonable perspective, and I have certainly met people where this isn't immediately obvious, but it's not the whole picture in its entirety, either. I got into therapeutic community work because I was a baby born in an era of post-conflict violence. When I take the time to explore the wisdom in my body, it is still teaching me how to sensitively navigate traumas in myself and others at almost forty years of experience.

I was once told that your approach to pregnancy indicates how you'll approach parenting. So, being mindful during pregnancy is a really good opportunity to gain insight into the space that you want to create as a parent. This enables you to make decisions authentically instead of feeling like you're just reacting or falling into the habitual cultures and wounds of your own upbringing.

It's worth remembering that no two children or parents are the same. If there were a manual, a single correct way of doing everything, it would be a bestseller. But there isn't. We're all doing our best with what we have in each moment. Knowing the excruciating detail of what some of us have been through, I think we're all doing incredibly well!

Chapter Sixteen

Being Seen, Heard & Felt

Fast-forward to summer 2018. I was teaching yoga part-time in a local studio, mothering a thriving two-year-old, and leading two voluntary community music collectives.

When my son was born, I quickly realised that I would need some "me time" activities outside of the home where I could let go and do something that energised me. I set about creating some ukulele groups where I could enjoy practising music, push myself a little further and build communities around my newfound desire to liberate my voice. As I've already mentioned, when my son was just two months old, he attended his first ukulele festival, where I performed a solo set and as part of an ensemble. This deadline for my solo performance made me create boundaries and ringfence time for creativity and practice. Anyone who sings will tell you it requires a degree of breathwork, which inevitably improves your mental and emotional states. So, these projects ultimately made me a healthier version of myself and a better mother and wife. It is often the case, especially for women and mothers, to see this time as a luxury. Typically, these kinds of indulgences are the first to go when we feel overburdened and start looking for what has to give to accommodate life's twists and turns.

In March 2020, when the global pandemic hit, I took advantage of the circumstances after the initial shock of it all. With Skinner furloughed and me categorised as "at risk" with an underlying respiratory condition, the advice was to stay home. Within two months, I had organised and created a world-first, three-day online ukulele festival. It was a roaring success through which international relationships were forged and still endure.

I taught yoga online, did live stream classes and videos, podcasted some meditation lessons, and just enjoyed playing around with the potential of being internationally available. Some of the things I enjoyed the most were co-hosting singing and beatboxing workshops with my very dear friend Julius! Due to the world's online nature at that time, I also met and worked with his wonderful fiancée, Klaudia. It was such a difficult time for so many people, but I was able to mine many golden opportunities from the rubble.

One such opportunity was volunteering with and later working for The Embodiment Conference. A good friend of mine, Natalie, had put me onto them as they were running yoga sessions online, and she shared the links with me, thinking I would be interested. Later in 2020, they planned to host the world's largest-ever education event online; they worked in the online education sphere long before the global pandemic was on anyone's radar. With my background in Community Development in the Community Voluntary Sector, I saw an opportunity to assist with the conference as a volunteer Charities Coordinator. I put my name forward and, soon after, assisted the core team in researching and implementing a policy on social responsibility. In typical Róisín style, I also studied every aspect of what they were doing, how and why. I don't know what drew me to understudy the conference in this way, but I was intrigued and found the insights worth the energy spent.

I know that if Skinner hadn't been furloughed at the time, there's simply no way I could have participated like this due to being the primary caregiver to my son. Still, since he could not work and was confined to the home full-time, I could engage at very short notice and suddenly found myself very generously invited to participate in the core teams' four-week pre-conference 'Peak Performance Training.' Each week consisted of six Systema Sessions, one Non-Violent Communication session, one Embodied Coaching session, one Mindset Coaching session and one Meditation session for a whole month! It was, hands down, one of the most indulgent periods of focused personal development I have ever undergone, and I will be forever grateful to Mark and the rest of the core team for initially welcoming me in with open arms. Other members of the fifty-plus-strong team later became like family, too. The instructors on this four-week conditioning programme were out of this world, and I felt so grateful to have access to such community infrastructure and wisdom. The more I deep-dived into the field of embodiment, the more I realised that I had been immersed in this work for years without the accompanying language or discourse to describe it accurately. It felt like a coming home, which amused me as the conference strapline was "Coming home to the body." How fitting indeed!

In the months leading up to the conference, I attended many of their free online events and learned about my areas of interest and work. I considered presenting at the conference, and as I had worked over the last five years on the relationship between shame and my voice, I decided to create a session for the conference based on this topic. I applied to and was accepted onto the Dance & Creativity Channel, which spurred me to create and deliver a four-part online course on exactly that theme to test content and garner feedback for the online session I ran before the conference. The course and conference session were a resounding success and illustrated how I used my healing journey to empower and inspire others. This is what Stage Six of meditation, *Mission & Purpose* looks like. Once again, I found myself in a position where I was able to wade through a dark and desperate time, tune into a higher frequency and turn it into a personal period of post-traumatic growth. It felt like I was still harnessing and implementing the healing I could access through the Vipassana retreat and my time spent with Julius and looping it into another opportunity. It almost felt like the motion of a monkey swinging from vine to vine, riding waves of flight, timing my next catch perfectly to continue the momentum and not stall; yet it never felt like grasping or like forced circumstance; more flow than frenzy.

I have come to realise that when you are in the company of people who applaud your healing rather than resent and resist it, you encounter much less friction than what I had learned to expect as the norm during my teenage years.

So, during this Peak Performance Training, I was introduced to the chief instructor, Matt Hill, from

Systema Academy in Wiltshire. I attended almost every session and loved the variety of training across the weeks. No two sessions were the same, and I felt notably better after each. By the time the four weeks of training had ended, I felt strong and healthy. I had been avoiding training my core for years after my C-section. I was afraid of it, and after previous failed attempts to rebuild strength that led to injury and a mental aversion to even trying, I was surprised by what I had been able to achieve in four short weeks. The conference lasted for ten days, and there was no training during that time. Instead, I worked night and day behind the scenes on affiliate marketing emails, supporting the core team in any capacity and delivering my own session, which was an awesome experience. I even went to London to meet some of the crew in person. That was the cherry on the cake! About a month after the training ended, I decided that what I had been learning was worth pursuing. So, I reached out to Matt to find out if he was running any more online classes. And so began my official Systema Martial and Healing Arts training.

For the first year, I trained six times a week, all solo training online, per the ongoing COVID guidelines. I couldn't quite believe the depth of education and connection I was able to engage in via the online environment, and it further spurred me on to reconsider the business model I wanted to pursue as a freelancer and stay-at-home mum. The option of teaching online was becoming increasingly attractive as I became less fearful of the camera and of being seen.

In December 2020, I decided to take my studies more seriously and enquired about the route to becoming a Systema Instructor. I attended my first camp in April 2021 over my birthday weekend, which was during one of the first major relaxations of COVID regulations across the UK and Ireland in over a year. I absolutely loved training in nature and meeting the 3-D faces of people I had come to spend a lot of my time with over the previous twelve months. It felt very similar to the circus community I talked about at the start of this book. It wasn't that we were all the same, far from it, but there was a tangible, recognisable frequency that I knew I could feel safe and relaxed in.

I committed to submitting my first application for "Instructor-in-Training" for my one-year anniversary of training in September 2021. Ambitious, yes, but until now, I had only ever known Systema as a solo practice. As far as I was concerned, it was a practice I already knew how to teach, albeit in another language: yoga therapy, meditation, sound therapy, massage, and conflict resolution.

In reality, Systema comes into its own when you can titrate the experience and pressure-test your skills in the context of contact with others, typically through combat. I cannot believe how quickly some of the things that I have practised for years were just entirely unavailable to me when under certain types of physical or psychological pressure - like literally forgetting how to breathe just because someone was pretending (quite slowly) to come at me for an attack. To say it was humbling would be an understatement.

Before I completed the Mongol Rally, I had the opportunity to undertake the MTQ48, Mental Toughness Quiz, comprising forty-eight questions. I was told that I came out in the top 5% of candidates globally to the point where they wanted to interview me further to see how I perceive challenge, threat and success. I would love to see how Systema students around the world would fare in taking this quiz because I have never known this kind of training in all my sampling of various modalities and contexts across cultures in this lifetime. I suspect they would all do very well, such is the nature of the training.

When I broke my ankle in May 2021, I thought this would derail my plans to submit my Instructor-in-Training application. Still, it ended up being yet another transcendental episode of learning and training. To fully describe the context and depth of my revelations here and how they link to my previous eye-opening transitions, I will begin by taking you through my first group experience of Systema at the camp in April and how it coloured my understanding of pain relative to the physical experience versus the emotional and historical contexts.

So, in Systema, everything we train comes back to being relaxed. This isn't simply how *chill* you can be under pressure; it's a deep, intimate relationship with the state of your nervous system, psyche, muscular body and quality of your breath at any given point in time, dependent on the external factors of your environment; the emotional influences of your past and present experiences, and the cleanliness of your intent which you cultivate day to day (or not) through your habitual practices. To that end, I regard Systema as a meditation practice, a devotion to being intentionally pure of spirit, calm of psyche and soft in physical demeanour. That is not to say there is no fight in Systema; quite the opposite. One of the foundational principles, and the reason the United Nations Headquarters recognised it as the most humane contemporary Martial Art, was the commitment to "do the least harm," a principle with which I wholly resonated and later discovered originates from their Orthodox Christian roots.

So here I was, some five short years later, playing with training knives and bare-knuckle strikes, finally about to embark on the learning journey I had identified on my first day at the Vipassana retreat, learning to value myself as I valued all other living creatures. To deliberately train the intention: "I am worth fighting for. I am a priority and as beautiful a creation as any other." Can you honestly speak these words about yourself and, more importantly, believe them? This was something I played around the edges with when I was singing Julia Michaels's song "Issues." I also remember trying to get through the lyrics of Christina Aguilera's song "Beautiful" back then, and could not sing them without my face contorting and my voice breaking. It took some dedicated practice to move beyond this, but I got there.

"That which you practise, grows; where your intention goes, energy flows."
Buddhist Teachings

In Systema, we practise physical interventions for self-defence, a concept that was entirely alien to me. These lessons were handed down through word of mouth, and there's no easy way to access the accompanying philosophical discourse, so I've had to formulate my own understanding of what justifies striking another being because my understanding to date was that you should just leave people to their actions and consequences, bearing responsibility only for your own conduct. My understanding is shifting as my practice evolves, but my interpretation then was as follows.

When someone seeks to harm and destroy, if it is within your gift to do so safely, then it is your duty to stop them, not only because they would harm another but also because, in the act of doing so, they would further inflict harm on themselves.

Consider someone who would stab a stranger for the sake of stealing their wallet. Not only is the theft taking them down a road of self-harm and a cycle of negative interactions with their environment, but the intent to use a weapon violently, to commit that premeditated assault on another living creature, would so gnarl and distort their psyche that they will find it harder and harder to heal and come back from such events to live in their true nature.

You might argue that to be aggressive and greedy is their true nature. However, in Systema, we describe this conduct as one of the many expressions of fear which constrict the body and mind, often in unrecognisable ways. Giving the benefit of the doubt, assuming that people are inherently good, unconditional love and positive regard are all practices I've known from other aspects of life. And they apply here too. It's better that we intervene to stop such events from ever occurring where possible, limiting the potential for the amount of damage. In other words, it is more responsible to intervene, if you can, and prevent any destruction that may ensue, than to turn a blind eye and allow whatever malice to play out unhindered. As I understand it, this is the ethical, moral and spiritual argument for physical intervention in a conflict or combat situation.

As you can imagine, my background didn't naturally lead me to a place where physical combat was ever a viable option. Coming from the perspective of mediation and conflict resolution, I would have generally understood that escalating any conflict to the point of physical engagement would mean that I hadn't done my job well enough. It took many hours of personal enquiry and practice to realise the frictions I was facing and bring them to the fore through my training, allowing me to consider and interpret them from new angles. We must train and prepare to ensure that when we act, it is always from a place of compassion, absolute sincerity and positive intent to remove tension and fear from our opponent rather than amplifying and aggravating the situation through our own, often unrealised worries, fears or prejudices.

To take this one stage further, when your body is rigid with stress and worry, it makes your actions brittle, sharp and destructive. You receive external pressure in a much more volatile, emotional and inherently damaging way. Conversely, when your muscle body is relaxed, your thoughts are clean (i.e. not full of resentment or worry), and the expectation of threat unburdens your nervous system, you can receive external pressure more detached and rationally; it becomes more like interpreting data than an experience of pain or conflict.

I was fully aware that I was missing a key piece of information in all of this. As I had mentioned earlier, I had given up my meditation practice for a while because it felt like self-harm, like I was actively creating the conditions for people to desecrate my mind, intentions and actions. So, understanding how to stand up for myself was a key aspect of beginning this work. I was relearning that there is a time and a place to inflict worldly, short-term pain or temporary discomfort on another (notice I did not use the words "harm" or "injury" here). I'm aware that sounds utterly bonkers. Don't worry; there's a lot more to it.

When I went to the camp and had my first experience of training strikes, I discovered that I had a lot of emotional baggage to unpack. We don't use gloves or pads for training as this removes us from our human attacker; rather, we work with the human body of another. We practise hand-to-hand combat and skin-to-skin interaction, feeling our way around the other person and their tensions, fears and limitations. If you can train with enough subtlety, it becomes a remarkably tender and humbling experience, sharing vulnerabilities, bathing old wounds, and casting light on once-hidden scars. Honestly, I was not expecting physical combat training to feel so profoundly spiritual or intimate, especially when you search Systema online, and all you find are videos of middle-aged dudes in camouflage gear making lots of noise and emptying gut punches into each other.

Whether you are training with the body, weapons, or solo with just your own breath, the aim is to constantly return to a baseline state as close as possible to that of receiving a massage as frequently and effortlessly as possible. For some people, Skinner being one of them, even the word "massage" makes them hold their breath and raise their shoulders in intense apprehension, so aiming for the same feeling as receiving a massage isn't necessarily a universal descriptor, but it's the best I've got.

As a yoga teacher, I trained for years to find that peaceful, serene state whilst holding a challenging pose. Through my meditation training, like with the thunderbolt pose in long, multi-hour sits, I learned that pain can be a figment of the monkey mind to pull my attention away from the universal truth of infinite oneness. Rather, that pain, the emergency signal your body sends when you are in danger, and suffering, the intersecting degrees of discomfort that you can experience in relation to an event, are two entirely different and distinct things for which we have conflated the words and descriptions. I enjoyed training and was already familiar with these practices, so I could see how easily they transferred into my everyday life. They made me less easy to rile, more patient in challenging environments, and exponentially more rational even when triggered far beyond my capacity to reason or respond verbally.

The late Mikhail Ryabko, founder of modern-day Systema, teaches that you can see malicious intent, fear and pain in another by how they hold themselves and even in observing their breath if you are sensitive and close enough - often before they've even cognitively decided to lash out or fight. The earlier you can identify these tensions in another person, the more options you have to disperse or remove them before they spill over into physical aggression. We study drills like holding a training knife, noticing how it affects the psyche and literally changes our physical inclinations. Does holding the knife embolden you? Do you instantly gather your muscles and lean forward? Do you begin to lose your relaxed, human empathy and relish the feeling of power? We must work to identify these things in ourselves before we can begin to recognise them in others. If we cultivate our experience with compassion, we can have a degree of human empathy for an attacker, knowing that we, too, are fallible and subject to the influences of fear.

With enough personal practice, we start associating this knowledge with where these tensions manifest in our bodies as physical symptoms. So if gripping the training knife makes my arm tense up to my bicep and shoulder, then the quickest way for someone to "take the fight out of me" is to remove the knife from me, whether by taking the weapon directly by disarming from my grip, or striking the muscles that I'm using to grip it. Think about it. Did anyone ever give you a dead arm in school? Or, having slept on your arm during the night, can you recall how utterly ineffective it was for a short time after? By adding a measured, precise, and targeted degree of external physical pressure such as this, we can effectively neutralise the imminent threat of danger while minimising the potential for it to reoccur in quick succession, as the tension that initially sought to fuel the attack no longer exists. It has been converted and exchanged, not destroyed; such is the nature of energy. Of course, there are other ways to subdue an attacker, no matter which weapon(s) they wield. This is just one example to illustrate the point.

Furthermore, one of the most fundamental things we explore in Systema is breathwork, specifically breath holds. A substantial part of this is understanding how quickly fear and panic enter the psyche and move into the muscular body when we hold our breath. Often, our initial reaction to any disruptive event is to hold our breath, even for a split second. Unintentional breath holds are a surefire way to bring tension, fear, and malice or "unclean thoughts" into the body, and it is likely that we are not aware of this trickling in. So, we train "continuity of breath" and "breath independence" whilst under pressure to ensure that we are constantly fuelling and cleansing the body and psyche when under attack, so that we don't go from a relaxed interpretation of incoming data to hysterical, reactionary, panic-fuelled mania when confronted with stressful situations.

By now, you are no doubt beginning to see how these skills and abilities translate very well to everyday life, enabling a quality of being that is above the normal functions or expectations of how we've been educated to live and thrive.

I went to my first camp with all the information I had garnered over the previous eight months of solo online training, and I pressure-tested it in this group setting. This appears quite unique to Systema and certainly isn't something I've come across through my yoga teacher training. Throughout the weekend, we trained in relaxed movement, balance, night training, cold water dousing, and partner combat with sticks. The camp training was delivered with a degree of social distancing in small groups, even outdoors. We slept in hammocks and cooked our food over the campfire, and I couldn't have felt more at home. It felt like next-level learning progressions for my previous studies, upping the ante to broaden and deepen my understanding. Cossack whips weren't on my radar before this camp at all, and they were first mentioned when Vaz, Sam and I were talking about piercings and tattoos. Degrees of pain and discomfort and how everyone related to those experiences very differently. Vaz described a Cossack session with Vladimir Vasiliev and said he might ask Matt to do one at camp. I didn't think any more about it.

Sometime later, we did a two-hour workshop on Systema massage in pairs, sometimes described as "warrior massage," one typical practice is using the feet. One person (the receiver) lies on the ground while the other person applies degrees of pressure through the receiver's muscles using various parts of the soles of their feet. The receiver's job is to manage the incoming pressure using their breath. It is the job of the person giving the massage to monitor the receiver's breath and adjust accordingly to help clear pockets of tension. Towards the end of this session, Matt offered a whip massage. There was zero expectation or pressure for anyone to participate. When the offer was made, I put my hand up to take part. Still, Helen, a very experienced practitioner and female instructor who I was massaging at the time, insisted that I watch the demonstration before committing to anything. A Cossack whip is a leather, nearly metre-long, plated whip reinforced with a steel rod in the centre and a concealed metal bearing or bullet in the tip. It has a chunky handle with a looped strap.

The demonstration, right beside where I was working, looked scary but doable. I've no idea how many people went ahead of me, and I don't remember much about waiting for my turn other than concentrating on finishing the remainder of the partner massage. I do remember commenting to Helen that I wasn't sure what was scarier, the crack of the whip as it whizzed through the air or the expostulations of those being struck! These were not superficial welts. When it was my turn, I moved into the sun from my spot in the shade and asked what I was meant to do. "Small movements like we do in class and burst breathe," was the concise explanation.

Lying face down, there were three passes on the back of the body, just like the massage: first pass – touch, second pass – weight, third pass – pressure/force. Each pass had two parts: tapping using the whip looped over, followed by using the full length of the whip. I can barely remember the first pass, but it undoubtedly let me find a rhythm and relax into what was to come. I have since wondered if I would've handled it the same if I hadn't just had the most incredible massage from Helen. There were about a dozen lashes with the length of the whip per each pass. The second pass spiked some fear in me, and

I clenched the muscles in my low-mid back just before impact. Well, I definitely felt that one! I instantly realised that relaxation and focused breathwork would be the easiest way. I felt ready for the third pass. Determined to stay soft and focused, I settled into a pattern, exhaling on impact to gently initiate some movement, then burst breathing to clear residual tension before inhaling to coast through the next impact. I remember Matt saying, "Nearly there," about halfway through the third pass. Each lash landed with a searing, stinging heat, which dissipated surprisingly quickly. When it was over, Matt said, "You did incredibly well there. Real warrior spirit." My first thought was, "I'm sure everyone is told the same thing."

The instruction was to lie and enjoy the heat, but I couldn't find any heat. I began shivering. It wasn't like trauma tremors or adrenaline shakes. I just felt cold, like with the warrior massage earlier, which was why I'd moved into the sun before we began. I didn't have any striking revelations during the session, but I noted the irony of saying, "It feels like I've forgotten how to be strong" around the campfire later that evening, as this is clearly not the case.

However, this session did more than make me feel strong. It rewired how my brain interprets physical sensations of pain. From my earlier understanding of pain through the Vipassana retreat, I was able to tap into a place where I wasn't emotionally involved with the incoming experience. By focusing on my breath during the session, I could stay remarkably clean in my thoughts, and the small movements allowed me to shake off any pockets of muscular tension, which helped keep the sensation of impact less antagonistic. And so I began to understand how we, especially in Western culture, are taught to cultivate a relationship with the physical experience of pain, which is largely founded on fear, emotion and a lack of trust both in our own capacity to handle it and in the intentions of others.

I returned home from camp, and I don't know why I was surprised to see huge bruises all over my back. That worried me. How would I explain to Skinner, or anyone else for that matter, that I lay down, of my own free will, and allowed someone to do this to me? It sounded a bit like, "Yeah, this guy I met online, well, I followed him into the woods, and he beat me with a whip, and we're training again tomorrow night" - it sounds a bit crazy, right? And yet, my husband, through his own understanding of physical activities and competitive sports, didn't react massively. He understood that injuries occur in contact sports, that temporary, superficial wounds are part and parcel of some experiences, and that it's possible to come home bloody and scraped and not feel victimised by the experience, as he had done weekly throughout his entire life playing field hockey on a shale surface! He asked if I would do it again, and I said I wasn't sure. True to form, he was his usual, supportive, patient and understanding self.

It's worth stressing that context is everything. If I had come back looking fragile, sounding broken, detached, flinching or worse, he might have had cause for concern. But that wouldn't accurately describe the state I arrived home in.

Over the coming days, I experienced some serious grounding and therapeutic catharsis, which I put down to several things: the amazing visceral massage I received from Helen, the eight months of almost daily training I had done before arriving at camp, being in physical proximity to people again after so long in lockdown and, of course, the whip massage. If I had gone into it with a different mindset and felt like I was being punished or deserved to be hurt, harmed, or humiliated, it could've been an altogether different and perhaps even negative experience. If I had endured it despite fear and resentment, I think it could have been the end of my martial arts training and an easy reason to feel sorry for myself. Instead, it felt like a realignment, an adjustment that went far beyond the everyday muscle massage and deep into the nervous system, psyche and soul. I'm still unsure whether achieving such states without physical intervention is possible, but I expect so with dedicated practice and the right teacher. Indeed, I had touched the edges of this truth before through a strict, seated meditation practice. However, I think this is still very much a physical experience which requires some tactile engagement with pain to obtain such a degree of clarified oversight.

When I think about the images I've seen of competitors' faces after an MMA or boxing fight, I've always wondered why they would pursue such blood-thirsty sports. I never really understood how they could go through something like that and still want to compete again. It's not something that has ever appealed to me, and while it doesn't feel like these are the same lessons, those images of bruised eyes and busted noses are mainstream across our media platforms. There must be something that these athletes have learned about the decipherable strands of the experience of pain and the inherent sense of resilience and strength gained from realising we're not as frail as we're taught to believe, which allows them to continue in their careers and keep chasing those title bids. Even in circus arts, we interact with the experience of physical pain, knowing that it is a temporary pitstop on the way to proficiency and progression, from dancing with hula hoops, climbing ropes barefoot or lying on a bed of nails.

The whip treatment, however, reminded me more of watching old kung fu movies where they punch blocks and boards until their knuckles bleed. I found myself thinking this was just a niche learning threshold typical of any martial arts training, with very illuminating lessons around the true nature of our human body, how robust we really are in our physicality, and how much we are steered towards the illusion of comfort in the modern era, which seeks only to dull our senses and prop us up on crutches; making us more reactive while simultaneously less effective.

It is worth stating that, despite the use of whips, chains and other improvised weapons when training Systema, this is not kink. If you're thinking of heading to your nearest Systema class hoping for fetish gear and swingers' parties, you'll be massively disappointed. However, upon discussing some of the potential learning outcomes with sexologist friends and those who take an experimental approach to pleasure-seeking activities, it seems that there is an opportunity for similar therapeutic realisations of the self and a tending to old, previously rejected parts of the self, that is accessible through either and both practices. Actually, *Shibari*, the decorative and aesthetic art of rope tying, and *Kinbaku*, the art of bondage, both originate from the ancient Samurai martial arts practice of *Hojójutsu*, which was a way of tying captives to restrain, transport and even torture them. So, there is some distant connection in that sense.

I thought it was worth highlighting this because we tend to avoid the unknown all too often in life, aiming instead to keep on the side of familiarity. Still, as I found out with meditation, life is just a spiral, looping back repeatedly to the same lessons. In my quest for understanding spirituality, I learned that most expressions of faith are the same feeling described in different languages with a central aspect of surrendering to a greater source, energy, God, chi, prana, 'the universe' or however else you might describe it. Returning to the same lesson shouldn't feel like failure; it's the nature of the path. The work is to direct your response in line with your values and virtues. Each time you revisit an experience, sometimes known as a trigger, it's an opportunity to observe if you can access a different reaction and change the trajectory. If the answer is "no," that isn't meant to be some judgement on you; it's just an indication that it's possible to move more from where you are in that moment.

Hopefully, through sharing these stories, you'll be able to see how, at times, it has taken me years to find the right opportunity or practice to address old constructs, habits and hurts. There's no race to the finish line, no accolades or awards ceremonies. There's just you on your path. Your quality of life and whether or not that extends beyond you into the lives of those around you. We all have much more influence on the world around us than most of us are aware of. And when we wield our influence in ignorance, we have the potential to do untold damage. As I can see now, the concept of surrender has as many different modalities and languages to describe this feeling as there is an infinite number of opportunities to experience it.

Everyone will have their own entry point for meditation, and similarly, what one person views as a fairly mainstream practice, another might regard as completely beyond comprehension. I've concluded that it's not fundamentally relevant which modality you practise, so much as the intention with which you practise that's important. The rest is just a framework so that you can relate it to the common, predictable experience of others and feel assured that you are on the right track.

Chapter Seventeen

Break a leg

When I broke my leg a few short months later, it was a most peculiar experience. At the top of the slide, I had a sudden inkling that it was not a good idea to go down it and that I could break a limb. I ignored that thought, set my son on my lap and by the time I got to the bottom of the slide, I had fractured my ankle. With my son sitting on my knee in a confined, covered-over space, I had nowhere to go. For a split second, as my ankle got caught and my body kept moving forward, I thought, "Oh wow, all this obscure-angle mobility training we've been doing is really paying off. I might get away with this," and then "pop!" There was the unmistakable noise of bone snapping. When we got to the bottom of the slide, I quickly removed my boots and waterproof overalls before my ankle began to swell. I got my son to carry my waterproofs up the hill to the car as I made my way up on three legs like a wounded animal. By the time we got back to the car, I knew I couldn't press the pedals to drive us home and resigned myself to call for help.

I kept a training journal for the next two months and will share extracts that help illustrate some of the learning outcomes around fear, pain, and the power of breathwork. I appreciate that many people live with and manage enduring and chronic pain, and I'm not for a second trying to speak to those experiences. I've never been in that position, and I wouldn't dare assume to know what it's like. I am not saying these are universal experiences of injury or physical trauma, far from it;

however, they are my accurate and authentic insights. They are an indication of what's possible when you can decipher your experiences and observe without precondition and emotional attachment.

I decided to skip training that first night. My leg was in a Plaster of Paris cast, and I was trying to fathom how I would hobble around looking after my hyperactive toddler for the next few weeks. I started back to training again the very next day and continued to train six times a week with one leg in a cast from toe to knee for the coming eight weeks. Having moved very little in the twenty-four hours since the injury, I was surprised to find how accessible some of the training was when I returned the next day. The training topic was "Managing Fatigue," and I noticed how consciously minimising tension in my body allowed me to protect the injury while maintaining a surprising degree of mobility and freedom in my body. I noticed my ankle throbbing but *without* pain towards the end of the session and was reassured to feel how the injury was receiving a fresh flush of oxygenated blood. I noted how optimistic I felt about training with an injury for the next two months. Later that evening, I attended another class and observed how relaxed my leg had felt all day.

Notably, the only time I have felt pain in the injury is when I have tensed up the leg trying to prevent a fall, and once when I also mindlessly landed on my injured foot to stop myself from falling over. I'd been wondering about how relatively pain-free the whole experience had been to date, and I put a lot of that down to all the dedicated breathwork and movement training I'd done before the injury: a combination of conscious-directed breathwork and intentionally keeping the muscular bodies, psyche, and nervous system relaxed. I knew the whip massage was in some way relevant to all of this, but at that time, I was still unravelling how. That's the thing about exploring life through a spiritual lens; as we have touched on so many times already, most of the time, you won't have an explanation for what you're experiencing; you'll just know how it feels.

Later that afternoon, I did some gentle ground movements, including sit-ups, push-ups, and leg raises. I realised that the previous night in training, I had learned to do sit-ups without tension in the legs, which is a distinctly Systema movement. This had been key to helping me move pain-free, i.e., without unnecessary aggravation of the limb. While doing the push-ups, I felt stronger and still somehow much weaker at the same time. The leg raises are so enjoyable, and after the first few, when I brought my injured leg back to rest on the ground, it felt almost cold with tingles and sensations, like opening the window in a stuffy room, flushed with freshness. I did a few more leg raises, concentrating on raising my legs above my head using my breath and focusing on softening my back muscles. I've found much more freedom in leg raises since the visceral massage at camp. But this particular day, with the weight of the cast overhead, the feedback from the floor against my body felt different, and I was able to use muscle relaxation to change the direction of the leg raise, as well as by using the breath. I found the quality of training I could enjoy with such a dominant limitation remarkable, and the insights really accumulated over the coming weeks and months. The balance training we'd been doing sporadically in class had given me a level of embodied confidence that, I think, terrified Skinner to watch! It wasn't long before I was doing standing-to-ground transitions without hesitation despite being one limb down.

In terms of psychological stress throughout this experience, the pinnacle was self-administering daily Clexane blood- thinning injections at home. Since both my age and BMI were over thirty, I was at risk of blood clots with my lower limb injury. The last time I was in this situation, I was post-op emergency C-section, and my body reacted with immense dread and pain, as I've described. I had only six days of injections to do in the previous instance and thought I'd never be able to get through it, so upon hearing that I had six-plus weeks of daily injections to manage, I was struggling not to hold my breath.

On Day One, I wasted two doses trying to administer them without taking the safety cap off!! When I saw how far off my diligently curated relaxation baseline I was, I breathed, phoned the nurse, had her talk me through it and finally got it done. The next day was much easier. A few breaths and it was all over in seconds. There was very little mental pushback at all! After that, it became like brushing my teeth or any other daily routine.

I do not doubt that the confidence I'd gained in training with this injury, plus seeing how remarkably effective the breathwork was in overcoming fear and regulating my nervous system responses, helped me to tackle these tougher historical and psychological challenges too. I noticed how calm and relaxed I could be through these conflicts and knew these practices were ultimately supporting my family (and now primary caregivers) through this stress-inducing experience too.

Over the last year's training, I noticed that I'd been letting small amounts of stress accumulate, sneaking in and gradually piling up. So, during my recovery, I consciously went into my body to clear out tension using burst breathing periodically throughout the day, even and especially when I didn't feel stressed. I was staggered at the tension I, or rather, the breath, was finding and releasing. I make this distinction because I could feel that I wasn't directing the breath. I didn't know where the tension was at times, and yet, no matter how relaxed I felt, I was always able to disperse pockets of tension with my breath any time I simply undertook this breathing practice. I would feel the release and note that I had no awareness of that tension in my body prior to releasing it.

By the beginning of Week Two, I felt fatigued in my shoulders and chest from the impact of weight-bearing on crutches. I also realised about this time that while I'd been massaging the injured leg all week; the right leg, which was now working twice as hard to carry me around, hadn't been getting any attention at all, so I did some compression massage on the upper legs and knees with fists then went for a roll around on the floor. I focused mainly on leg raises but enjoyed using this to massage my back too, especially around my right shoulder blade. If you understand how to use a foam roller to self-massage dense muscle, you can quickly pick up how to use the floor to self-massage in much the same way. For me, this has been one of the biggest benefits of training Systema.

I used to think that making sounds when getting up off a chair or going to the floor was a way of letting out pressure, and it is, in some way, but it needs to be done consciously to have that effect, and it rarely is. Practising moving without making these sounds, however, will make your body and muscle tone more supple. More than that, being comfortable on the ground removes much of the fear around contact and falling, fears that generally increase as you get older. So, these are practices for a healthier and happier life no matter your age.

It's worth highlighting at this point that even if the only Systema you ever trained in was breath independence, that would drastically enhance your quality of life outcomes. Not everyone will train with weapons. Not everyone will participate in the combat classes, and that's ok. But the things you can learn through temporary discomfort, particularly in a world which seeks to infantilise us, pandering to the global rise in mindless consumption and superficial comfort-seeking, is actually mind-blowing. And yoga teachers, I'm sure, will relate to that sentiment.

One of my favourite cues in a yoga class is the instruction to "ease into discomfort," so this concept was not new to me, despite how bizarre and incompatible weapons training may appear to be when coupled with a commitment to non-violence.

Chapter Eighteen

Reflections on Pain and Fear

What did I learn from the first seven days in a cast? I learned that, in the right conditions, the mind's interpretation of pain can be reprogrammed and minimised, if not entirely eradicated. I have had some eye-opening experiences which have entirely unravelled my perceptions of pain whilst reminding me of lessons learned and only partially integrated some years previously. This injury has clarified my understanding of pain or pains as various strands of overlapping stimulation of the mind, body, and spirit, intersecting with the past, present, and future.

The felt sensation of physical pain is influenced, amplified and exacerbated by the experience of and relationship to other instances of pain, injury, affliction, harm and suffering across your lifetime. I can describe a few examples of fear and pain and how they've manifested in my body (or not) to help identify some individual strands of perception. Throughout my first week of recovering from my broken ankle, I had been pretty much pain-free since the injury occurred and even, oddly, *as* it occurred. I am told that is not the typical experience with a fracture, but it's decades since I'd had any comparable experiences. I can pick out precisely the instances when I felt pain across the week and count them on one hand. They can be attributed to circumstantial/ environmental incidents and sensory stimulation as opposed to the experience of discomfort or inflammation in muscle, joint or bone. I knew by the time I crawled back to my car that I would have to go directly to the hospital. There were no tears or distress. I just joked with my son as we waited for some help to arrive, and that was it. No drama. No reaction or pain or anything really of note, except the absence of these things.

My first encounter with pain in relation to this injury was after I had dropped my son off and my father took me to the hospital. I felt relieved, embarrassed, and momentarily teary with a touch of self-pity. Quality breathing soon got me over that.

The second instance was when the nurses were manipulating my limb and joints at the hospital, i.e. where I was neither in command of my mobility nor able to initiate it with my breath. I promptly asked the nurses to stop, give me instructions on how my limb should be positioned, and then allow me to manoeuvre myself. They were happy to oblige, and this made a huge difference to the experience as I was able to do whatever they asked without it taking an extended amount of time, but I was able to feel and manage the sensations in my body as they arose, which the nurses obviously couldn't. Perhaps most importantly, I could initiate movement with my breath, which then covered the movement and minimised tension and fear proportionate to my needs.

The next episode of pain was when I almost fell over, and I automatically put my broken limb out to save myself! This was unexpected, and it really hurt. As well it should have. It was a warning signal from my brain not to bear weight on this limb. I regained my balance and got seated comfortably, and moments later, after some directed breathwork, the sensations subsided. Actually, the mental discomfort and emotional worry of what had just happened in this instance hung around for hours afterwards. This made my leg feel restless and agitated but not sore. This minor incident knocked my confidence. I felt stupid and incapable, and it made me want to give up trying to move (this was still the day that I broke my ankle). I was concerned that I had done more damage. With it being a spiral fracture, it had the potential to continue to split further up or down along the bone. I thought that I had moved the goalposts since having the cast put on my leg, and now, potentially, I might have to have my leg broken again and reset. Well, that escalated quickly... in my head! Breathe!

In meditation, we talk about *Duḥkha* which relates to the experience of suffering. Other words I've used to describe it throughout this book include tension, friction and discomfort. However, with the experience of *Duḥkha*, the Buddha also cautions against "the second arrow," describing how it's not the initial instance of suffering which causes the most damage; it's the emotional wound of being injured that takes over and becomes the focus of our lament. When we pour our attention into generating and sustaining anguish over past events, they will torment us for as long as we continue to provide the fuel. My thoughts quickly escalating into panic is an example of the second arrow. The initial knock to the injury was negligible, but the fuel that I, or rather my ego, heaped onto the fire immediately after served to do nothing other than fan the flames. You can see how if I'd let these thoughts run unchecked, I'd have been an emotional wreck by the end of the day. If you don't know how to change your thoughts, you have several options: breathwork, movement or vibrationally (be that vocalising such as singing, chanting, talking, laughing, crying, or listening to music). When you change your internal situation, it changes your thoughts. It's worth noting that nutrition can also have a huge impact on the quality of your thoughts, as can sleep hygiene, so there are many variables you can play around with. However, one of the quickest and arguably most effective interventions I have found is breathwork.

The next experience of pain was similar. I was on the move again a few hours later, still on the same day. I almost fell again, but this time, I didn't put my foot down to save myself, and my awareness went straight to my arms instead. How do I break my fall?! In the split second when I realised that my arms were stuck in crutches and they were not going to be able to help me, I was scared! I felt hopeless, and *that pain* was intense. To be clear, I hadn't knocked or touched my injury from the outside, but a physical sensation of pain coursed through my entire body. It was searing hot and felt like all my nerve endings were on fire. A global sensation which seemed to emanate most intensely from the injury site. I acted quickly with an open mind to restore my posture and balance, using the breath. To my surprise, as soon as I intervened, the pain subsided. I didn't expect that because when it started, it felt like the sensations could overwhelm me and then, as if I had flicked a switch, it was over. Stopped. Gone. Did that really just happen?

You might say, "Of , the pain didn't last; you didn't actually hurt yourself at that point," but the pain I experienced in that moment was real, consuming. I didn't experience sensations like that even when I snapped the bone. I've no doubt that if I'd shrunk and contorted my posture, tensing my whole body to brace myself and protect the injury whilst also likely holding my breath, I would've created the optimum conditions for pain to thrive on varying levels and at multiple degrees of veracity.

At this point, I'll stress that I was not on strong pain medications or otherwise. Other than the two Paracetamol I was given when I arrived at the hospital I'd only taken a few precautionary over-the-counter Paracetamol at bedtime in case I tried dancing in my sleep or anything. Throughout the day, I was not taking nor requiring pain relief. I was still training, sometimes two or three times a day. So what was going on here? I wasn't entirely sure, but here are some observations I made.

It feels like psychological discomfort will break me quicker than anything I could physically endure. It feels like fear automatically compounds and exacerbates the physical experience. Well, more accurately, it feels to me like fear dominates and drives the experience.

There are more subtle curiosities to unpack. For example, bone pain and inflammation around the injury should cause a general and constant dull physical pain for at least the first week or two. So, where was that? I believe it was down to several things.

Directed breathwork

This helps reduce inflammation at the injury site and throughout the whole body, minimising cortisol production while also keeping the mind clear and the nervous system calm and soothed.

Conscious Tension Removal/ Muscle Relaxation

As a Musculoskeletal system, the body is full of levers and pulleys. Therefore, movement in one area of the body automatically and deliberately mobilises other body parts. Consider a sneeze and all the involuntary movement that it produces. We are finely balanced and wholly interconnected! You might assume that pain is inevitable when moving with injury but you can mitigate unnecessary friction, aversion and further inflammation in and around the injury by understanding anatomical function, being able to switch muscles on and off at will, and by using the breath to initiate and direct movement. These practices allowed me to manage the injury and the likelihood of a physical experience of pain minute-by-minute, movement-by-movement.

Cossack whip at April camp

I commented repeatedly when I broke my leg that there was no pain, and I started to get the impression that either people didn't believe me or couldn't grasp what I was talking about. It almost felt like I was talking another language. I'm sure that my relationship with pain and affliction has changed from this experience for example, at no point did I require pain relief to get me through the day, nor was I overwhelmed by sensations or thoughts of despair/lack of capacity to cope; and even comparable experiences like self-administered daily injections have been effortless. There was, of course, some friction at times, but for the most part, it was easily overcome and, at times, even proved productive.

So, I carried on training with one leg in a cast. I attended an online class led by Vladimir Vasiliev, themed “Invisibility & Weapons.” I noticed on Saturday's Zoom lesson there were two questions put to Vladimir asking about training with an injury, and I think Valerie said both questions came from the UK, which was funny to me because I didn’t ask either of those, so I was curious to know who did. In his answer, Vladimir said the best way to teach someone with an injury is to get the whole class to train as if they had the same injury, and I thought, 'Yes!' So I was hopeful for some groundwork challenges, and novel, playful, accessible movement in the following week's classes. Instead, I got multi-limbed, dynamic, complex movements, covering action within movement! It felt like I got everything I couldn’t do thrown at me that first morning. At times, I was uncharacteristically frustrated by it and was almost derailed by my own little pity party along the way, and yet, I gently and patiently nudged myself beyond where I thought I could safely go. By the end of the session, I had much smoother standing-to-floor transitions, was balancing on one foot in the middle of the room (moving away from the safety of walls or furniture that might break my fall), and even felt I could up the ante in how fast I could safely move with awareness.

Here's what I found most interesting. By that point, I had spent a lot of time considering pain and fear. I thought I had a decent handle on it and was surprised to find that there were multiple things I could do and access in these sessions that I was initially deeply hesitant to try, e.g. seated, half lotus-to-floor transition, which requires external rotation of the limb (i.e. applying pressure on and through the injury); moving quickly (as I thought this would be too rough/high impact); fast seated-to-supine transitions and fast standing-to-floor transitions whilst also drawing and concealing a weapon. Indeed, the more I consider fear and pain in relation to my injury and, more broadly, the more I realise there are ever more subtle layers of the same, the deeper I enquire. Such patterns are infinitely demonstrated through meditation practice, and these universal truths bear out time and time again across modalities that ultimately deepen our understanding of the fundamental principles of consciousness, life and love.

Even though I attended the following weekend's training, I didn't do a lot of movement due to much of the class being focused on renewing instructor certifications, and I noticed the negative impact staying stationary had on my psyche. I watched my mood decline over the weekend as I grew more restless, anxious and agitated. The less I moved, the more fearful and frustrated I became. I know this sounds obvious since we all know very well that exercise is good for mental health, but having done a lot of work with people who have physical limitations and complex mobility issues, this took on a vastly new meaning for me.

Move if and however you can, even if it is just to gently wobble your body like a bowl full of jelly as you lie in bed. This type of movement is actually incredibly therapeutic and can begin to teach your body to move more efficiently with less exertion. It keeps fear and frustration at bay and will allow you to dissipate incoming day-to-day aggravations, e.g. receiving bad news, intrusive thoughts or muscular tension like cramps and knots.

Move to minimise the experience of pain. It doesn't need to be vigorous or even travelling; it can be on the spot to access the benefits.

Systema is one of the most popular practices I have ever come across for people who are rehabilitating from extreme injury and trauma, from vehicle collisions to firearms wounds, neurological and biological disease, mental ill health and physical injury; its application is the closest thing I have seen to a truly inclusive and universal practice no matter your ability. If you can breathe, you can train!

I had a follow-up appointment with my consultant at the Fracture clinic, and he was surprised to hear that I hadn't been using any pain relief for the injury and was still regularly training with it.

I've been calling Systema "pressure-tested yoga," but it extends far beyond that. I learned to hone my awareness despite increasing degrees of stress. Other observations I made included noticing when I saw "new movement" in class, more advanced yet playful primal movement, and things that I wanted to try, like step-throughs and arm balances. I was quite envious, watching others and felt like I was missing out. In such scenarios, it's normal and easy to fall into a self-pity/victimhood mindset. I consciously tried to catch these thoughts as they arose because I'm only human, and of course, such thoughts came to mind. When I clocked them, I instantly flipped them with gratitude once more, as I've described a series of times now.

I trained in *Vladimir's "Three Levels of Weapons"* class online and really enjoyed it! After spending a week training in weapons with Matt online, I went into the class with the assurance that I could already handle it despite the cast. In journaling that, I remembered starting training Systema and recognised in that first instance how much I had missed the feeling of self-assurance, of a level of body confidence and competence that I knew could follow me anywhere. I am so grateful for these lessons, revelations and opportunities.

I have mentioned that my training has been helpful in my daily life, supporting my family and managing stress. Using the lessons from the fatigue and energy sessions, I could do shower time and bedtime stories with my son while managing a relatively new and pretty limiting injury. It is in these real-life scenarios where the training really shows its value.

Most people, professional fighters aside, don't train in self-defence to be a badass martial artist. They train to improve their quality of life outside of the training hall. It's essential to have the mobility, freedom, and dignity to advocate for oneself, engage openly with the people you love, and keep self-pity at arm's length. If these things go unchecked, they fester, colour, and distort your mood, manifesting in muscle tension, sabotaging your breathing, your structural integrity, and your access to creativity and intuition. When you are in a state of relaxed awareness, you can bring consciousness to aspects of your life which usually simmer under the radar, waiting for the tipping point.

Another example of this was training breath holds in class. I felt challenged by the very thought of it, so I instantly committed to a lenient approach. About halfway through class, I felt quite emotional and was briefly moved to tears. It reminded me of the recorded session I did during the Embodiment Conference when my aunt passed away. It felt like grief. Those heavy feelings could have been from watching *Gabor Matés' movie, "The Wisdom of Trauma,"* earlier in the day. The movement and breath holds we did in class helped clear some residual tension I hadn't realised I was harbouring.

Another application of breathwork I can describe was during my appointment with the fracture clinic earlier that same day. After removing the old cast, the consultant held my foot in place while the nurses put on the new cast. After looking at my x-rays, he explained that he would massage the calf bone back into alignment using his hands while flexing my foot towards me to correct a drop in the arch. I told him that I practise breath-directed pain management and asked him if he'd work with me on that, to which he agreed. I pre-emptively did two gentle rounds of relaxed burst breathing and was fine to stop. No pain. He seemed quite surprised. This was the same doctor from a few weeks before who was surprised I wasn't using pain relief. He got me to flex my foot by pushing it against his abdomen while he placed the heels of his hands on diagonal opposites of my ankle; the heel of one hand along the outside edge of my Achilles and the heel of his other hand pressed against the front inside edge of my shin bone, just above the ankle crease. I chatted away and could hear my vagal tone was totally relaxed. What I mean by that is that my voice and vocal tone were smooth, calm and mid-range. I wasn't high-pitched verging on tears or distress, nor was I agitated and poised for conflict at the apprehension of bad news. My voice was relaxed as if it was a normal situation with people I trusted. We've all had experiences of interpreting someone's vagal tone without knowing we're doing it; like when your friend on the phone says they're fine, and you know they're not, even though you can't see their face; or when you hear someone's voice quiver with nervousness; or when you walk into a room and know you've just interrupted an argument even though you didn't hear anything. These are all cues communicated non-verbally between one vagus nerve and another through our social engagement systems.

After a few minutes, we were finished, and I was sent off to x-ray again to ensure it was aligned for the next few weeks. I think seeing the reaction of medical professionals was one of the most interesting things for me throughout this experience. If I had been at home observing the healing and recovery, that would've been one thing, but recognising that the doctors were not seeing from me the usual symptoms of agitation, pain and fear which they usually associate with such an injury, based on their experience with what I can only guess is countless hundreds of patients, has once again affirmed the clarity I found in understanding the impacts of training, applied breathwork, muscle relaxation and a calm, clear psyche.

At times, I noticed that I was knocking into things with my cast at home or that my son would knock into me absent-mindedly. I observed how I grew in confidence each time I could rest without fear or reaction in these incidents. I felt mentally fortified by not reacting in fear, pain, and self-pity. I recognised it as the feeling of an ascending spiral, each incident fuelling the next level of progression and understanding.

About three weeks into training with the cast, we were doing standing-to-ground transitions around the clockface, prone, supine, either side and back to standing again. I regularly recorded my training sessions, as do many people these days. I found it amazing to watch the video from this class because it reminded me how scary the standing-to-ground transitions seemed in the first week of training with injury. Just three weeks later, because I gained the confidence to know that I could fall and roll safely if I lost my balance, I could comfortably do this multi-directional and at speed. I felt so happy that I kept up the training despite the limitation of injury, which points to something that I had struggled to name or fully understand. I questioned my strength for a few years, feeling like I was once strong, confident, and definitive. I could commit to a perspective, campaign, and worldview with full vigour and passion. Over the years of my meditation journey, I felt my strength had been lost or diminished, and I put it down to all those bruising, sometimes devastating experiences I'd had. But I was wrong. It is quite normal on the path of meditation that new, more nuanced outlooks can supersede former, more linear thought patterns. I used to be in awe of politicians, for example. I couldn't understand how they could commit a whole lifetime arguing with conviction that their perspective was right and that everyone else must be mistaken. But when you train to build empathy, compassion, patience and equanimity, it is quite understandable that the outworkings of that look much less like a one-track commitment to any particular agenda or campaign and very much more like the unconditional embrace of a loving mother. Training with this injury made me feel like my previous understanding of being strong was mainly just carrying unnecessary burdens, tension and fear. And when I let go of that, it made way for a myriad of less apparent yet inherently more universal strengths.

It feels like training in Systema has helped me identify and distinguish these qualities. Moreover, I now have the confidence, a (Stage Five) *Groundedness* in them, and hold them in as high a regard as the single-minded strength I previously thought I had. This made it obvious to me why I was drawn to working further with Matt, compared to the options of many other world-class instructors I had met during the Embodiment Conference.

Throughout the four-week peak performance training, we had access to experts in Yoga, Meditation, Breathwork, Coaching, Nonviolent Communication, Embodiment, Psychology - the list was endless. For some reason, I ended up choosing martial arts. No one was more surprised than me! I remember calling Matt "He-man" in one of his peak performance sessions because I was blown away by his apparent effortless strength, which was grounded in something more than muscle. I was drawn to develop these understated, relaxed, determined, and kind strengths, and Matt, much like my yoga teacher, Marie, modelled and mirrored those for me.

When I was setting out on my martial arts training around the time of the Embodiment Conference, I was struck by this quote:

"Power without love is brutality;
Love without power is ineffective."
Paul Linden

The second line really caught my eye. Through Vipassana meditation with the mosquito, I realised that I needed to redress my inner balance, and it is here I feel I have made the most progress in my training, especially through training with injury. Paul Linden is one of my greatest inspirations in understanding the potential and application of Trauma-informed Martial Arts. I didn't realise it at the time, but hearing about his work with survivors of gender-based violence and other devastating traumas would ultimately influence the trajectory of where I would take my practice and my work in Therapeutic Self-Defence. While still training with the cast, I attended Paul Linden's online session entitled *"Martial Arts in Trauma Recovery & Conflict*

Resolution." It was just what I needed to hear! He talked about how opening up to experiences actively diminished the sensations of pain and discomfort. I heard these words with new meaning, amplifying and echoing my recent experiences. When you have come to a fundamental realisation of what pain is, and everyone you raise it with disengages from the conversation, it is a relief to find someone who can talk about what you know as true and add context from their insights and lived experience.

Paul discussed the meditative axis and how to expand it intentionally. He emphasised that striking someone with only respect and kindness is appropriate. That way, you will only hit someone if they need it. This gave me comfort and confidence moving forward, as it makes sense and feels like something I can do since it's grounded in sensitivity work, compassion, and intention-setting, which I have cultivated and embodied for years.

Paul's martial arts background is Aikido, so this wasn't strictly Systema study. However, once again, the overlapping modalities of self-defence, coupled with my own knowledge of pranayama breathwork, meditation and yoga, all lead to the same ethos and practicable outcomes, forging my more objective understanding of universal truths relating to consciousness and the human experience. He elaborated on this by saying that to stay in the "vertical pole" or meditative axis (the space of expansiveness and universality) is the way, *or* structure**,** to ensure that you only ever hit with kindness and respect, which makes total sense to me now and compliments so much of what I hear and see in Systema classes the world over.

Coming from my non-violent conflict management background, I'm not embarrassed to admit that cultivating this perspective took me a couple of years to get my head around! It actually can't make sense unless you start to believe genuinely: "I am worth saving. I am a priority and as beautiful a creation as any other."

Paul covered many other things in that particular class, but something that really caught my attention was "lines of intention." He demonstrated with a student how, when resting his hand on the opponent's shoulder and trying to resist the opponent's efforts to remove his arm, he became closed, brittle, weak, and prone to injury. However, with his hand in the same position and, this time, intentionally reaching beyond the student's shoulder, it appeared to make the limb stronger and much more difficult to compromise. He wasn't using more force or creating more tension; he was visualising or intending to be more robust, choosing to be beyond or greater than the circumstances in front of him.

Let's run through that again; by simply visualising or intending to be more robust, by choosing to be beyond or greater than the set of circumstances in front of him, he was able to achieve a different state, to manifest a different set of circumstances. That is our inherent power if we learn to get out of our own way.

This last piece about lines of intention made an image pop into my head of me bursting a hole through the side of the slide rather than allowing it to break my leg. I suddenly realised that this is how Martial Arts masters of all kinds break through boards, blocks, etc., stuff we've all seen in countless movies, and for the first time, I felt that I could intrinsically understand where that power comes from. Moreover, these images and discourse subtly rearranged my understanding of the balance of tension required between total relaxation and maintaining an effective boundary of protection.

With all this enquiry around strength lately, I realised I hadn't lost strength, as I first thought; it was standing up for myself that I felt wholly incapable of. I appreciate that, from the outside, it doesn't look like I have difficulty with strength or standing up for myself, but internally, I've felt deeply ashamed in my life for not doing better, and that extends to a variety of incidents, some gender-based violence, some corporate bullying, and others where I thought I was amongst friends, only to find that it was nothing more than a mutual trauma bond; staying in company through perceived need and co-dependency from fear of rejection.

About two months into training with this particular injury, I realised that I had been re-introduced to a feeling of safety and security in my body that I barely recognised now as an adult. I could only identify it once it had returned, not in its absence. I felt so grateful to regain access to this part of myself. It also occurred to me that ***if*** the experience of physical pain, as I now perceive it, is some 80%+ emotional response, then we have the potential to inflict some grave wounds using only words or the absence of them. Therefore, this newfound strength of standing up for myself must be balanced with wielding my words as sensitively and respectfully as any other weapon I may choose. As I have misinterpreted this before, I thought it meant to say nothing at all costs, but this has sometimes been quite toxic and self-abusive. I now have a fuller sense of self-confidence, and whilst I would once again be comfortable in saying nothing/reacting less, it comes from an entirely different place. For the longest time, I thought being passive was achieved by meditating so hard that everything washes off you're your back. That no response or reaction is necessary, and certainly that can be true in the earlier stages of practice while you discern who you actually are, but when you get to a point where you trust your Self, your intuition, your gut and your instincts above anything else, then you discover that being passive isn't as hands-off as it sounds. Being passive is still holding a line, a boundary. And boundaries are important. My understanding of being passive now is to do everything possible to avoid conflict, but not at the cost of sacrificing myself. That's a completely different understanding and outlook to my initial interpretation, one that greatly improves my capacity for peace, relaxation and healing.

I asked a shaman recently about boundaries, telling him about my experience of feeling resourced by meditation, then later, feeling like it was inviting assault and abuse, and his answer was, "You need them until you don't." It took me months to figure out what this meant for me. As I now understand it, it's about the state of your nervous system. If you are in a dorsal vagal state, you need your boundaries. You need to practice all the meditation, chanting, breathwork and everything else that regulates your Vagus nerve so that you don't indiscriminately perceive everything as a threat. When you have moved into a regulated, ventral vagal state, you must continue your practice to maintain it. Still, your need for protective boundaries diminishes at this point because you'll no longer feel under attack from all angles. Even those who would seek to slight, offend or affect you would fail since your capacity to deflect such attempts would feel effortless, and that is how I have come to regard parts of my martial arts training now; as a practice in non-verbal boundary setting and defending.

One of the amazing things about training online during the pandemic has been the easy access to incredible international instructors. I was also enormously grateful to have trained with Victor during my recovery. When I attended his class around this time of reflection and enquiry, he began one particular session with his definition of strength: "Real strength is when your brain can send signals to *all* other parts of your body and receive feedback from them, fast." Man, was I ever so glad to have someone reframe and verbalise what I was trying to assimilate!

This is one of the primary reasons I study with and learn from a whole raft of teachers instead of being dedicated to one particular school of thought. It is all too easy to put the blinkers on and lean into the comfort of knowing, but, like any of the best lessons I've learned in yoga, meditation, sound therapy and more, what you learn internally on the mat, you must then be able to take out into the world. If it doesn't translate, it's simply a half-truth, delusion or distraction, a cute and reassuring construct that doesn't hold any weight but might make you feel better for a short time. So I love it when all the dots seem to magically connect when, for so long, the learning can feel like nothing more than an abstract paint spill.

An observation and reflection on letting go; that place, that feeling of surrender, was so familiar and accessible to me that part of me wondered if I had completely disassociated mentally from my body while being whipped. I questioned whether I had gone to a place where my body was intervening to prevent further trauma (this is something which is described and explained beautifully by *Stephen Porges's "Polyvagal Theory"* and is really valuable framing for those who perhaps berate themselves for freezing when under extreme and/or violent attack) but the truth is, I felt so present and in command of my faculties during that experience that disassociation doesn't seem to fit the description. Similarly, with not feeling anything as I broke my leg, I questioned how present I was, but I don't doubt for a second that I was wholly there and aware of what was occurring. I was not numbly avoiding, waiting for the experience to be over. If I hadn't witnessed this bizarre, pain-free injury, I would probably still be second-guessing all of this, but, to my understanding, all these experiences relate to each other in that it feels like the whip has hit a reset button on my pain receptors. I'm now reacting to pain in the same way that I've seen my three-year-old deal with injury, especially due to the lockdowns, as he'd had a very limited frame of reference or influence for how others usually react to pain.

It is remarkable to gain this perspective on our culture around pain, observing how the body and mind dutifully fill in the blanks of experience with expectation, memory and fear rather than accurately reflecting the real-time sensations alone. Fear and hopelessness eradicate the potential for joy, distort the truth, and keep us entrenched in patterns of mediocrity at best. Judgement narrows our options and leads to shame. Shame leads to trauma, and trauma leads to isolation, detachment and disconnection.

I'm not saying everyone should go and get whipped to cure all their ails, but I would encourage anyone to seek out their entry point and unashamedly embrace their practice. Pursue the things that make you feel energised, connected, and excited to draw breath and absorb what it is to be alive. Celebrate the body you've been loaned for your one wild ride on this giant rock as we hurtle through space and time - there will be no call for last orders before the final curtain falls.

Chapter Nineteen

Returning to the campfire

Throughout my studies, all my obscure and, at times, wildly unbelievable experiences, I have learned so many things about myself. To what end?

Two Picasso quotes lend themselves to the "What next?" question:

"The meaning of life is to find your gift; the purpose of life is to give it away."

and

"Inspiration exists, but it must find you working."

When I found myself sitting in a yurt at Into the Wild Festival in Sussex some ten years after I had first walked into the meditation experience at Sally Taylor's yurt, I was deeply moved by my journey and was very much looking forward to sharing that in full technicolour to the sell-out audience in front of me.

I was offering one of my now signature "Shame & the Voice" workshops, which had attracted fantastic reviews and acclaim over the last few years. When I deliver this workshop and see the tension drop from people's faces as they begin to relax, judge themselves a little less, and be more generous and gracious towards their inner parts, it reminds me of another underpinning quote:

"Shame cannot survive being spoken and being met with empathy."
Brené Brown

So I told my story, shared and led some of my favourite practices, moved people to tears, and watched people release their own ancestral baggage. I breathed a deep sigh of relief, observing how my story would become someone else's proof and inspiration. That my journey to radical self-acceptance, having waded through some utterly hostile and, at times, near-blindingly difficult episodes of self-doubt and enquiry, meant I could come back to the campfire and tell of my travels, to share my woes honestly and describe how I had overcome them, to offer hope that such a thing is possible, and to light the way for anyone else on a similar path.

I also participated in a "Soul Writing" workshop with Dr Sarah Walton at this festival. I knew I wanted to write this book to impart my lessons on releasing shame, overcoming creativity scars and owning your path, and I already had chunks of it drafted in my journal entries, but I didn't know how to bookend it. Since, through journalling, every time you externalise an experience by committing it to paper, you understand it a little better, it's hard to know where to stop the re-writes. Sarah's workshop was a testament to the fact that working with a guide or teacher who knows their craft can massively accelerate your learning. Much like all the other legends I've worked with and mentioned in this book, she offered some jaw-droppingly simplified insights gleaned over a lifetime's experience and mostly just held a safe space for me to realise that I had all the answers I needed all along.

The road of mindfulness can be blissful and deeply therapeutic in places. It can also feel troubling, confusing, and staggeringly lonely at times. Still, the gift of the journey, to know yourself and mankind on a level of commonality that is sorely lacking across the planet right now, is the ultimate quest, and I think it is worth every second. There are some common misconceptions about mindfulness-based practices: *The importance of learning to "Ease into discomfort"*

There is one thing I have found to be true time and time again: you must learn to face discomfort, working towards fostering as much equanimity as possible, whether that's making it through awkward poses, difficult thoughts, or challenging situations. When you don't habitually observe your thoughts, especially around the things that make you uncomfortable, you are often unintentionally and subconsciously creating the optimum conditions for pain, fear, illness, overwhelm and suffering to thrive.

Don't get conned into thinking that meditation will be your security blanket. For me, it has been more like a paint scraper, helping me peel back layers and layers of superficial ornamentation to reveal the true materials at play under the surface. You'll need to sensitively apply varying degrees of pressure to gain any revelatory experience, and it doesn't need to be extreme; the results will speak for themselves and be clearly visible to anyone paying attention.

When training in meditation or any other kind of introspective practice, it can be easy to become disheartened by succumbing to your emotions. Still, they are fertile ground for a whole wealth of learning. Admittedly, they may not help you remain level-headed amidst an attack or a car accident, so timing and choosing when to explore emotion is essential here. It is well worth dissecting your emotional responses if you are not in imminent danger. They are the symptoms of your competing internal parts, and when you understand them, you can choreograph how they interplay.

In the past, I gave myself a hard time for seemingly deep-diving headfirst into my emotions and untangling all the strands of stress and fear. I realise now that every cycle of enormous emotional toil and output has led me to a place of profound empathy. It has allowed me to come out the other side a little softer, even and especially when I hadn't believed such a thing was possible. So these days, I find myself standing back, observing the ebb and flow of emotion, realising that adding resistance and suffering to the ever-recurring nature of emotions is merely a distraction from the inescapable fact that emotions will come up, just like the sun, over and over again. To suppress them is short-sighted and delusional, as they will inevitably surface in some form. So get to know them. Get to know yourself. Most adults can only name four emotions, so out of touch we are with our internal landscape. Developing your emotional vocabulary and literacy will help you pinpoint what is at play, communicate more easily with others and avoid unnecessary friction, tension and misunderstanding, a skill we should all have and be taught in school.

Growing up during the 1980s and 1990s, a broad cultural theme of the music at that time was to tell people how much they mean to you while you can. This is something I do at every opportunity. Since I have come to perceive us all as little walking bundles of celestial magic, and as I have hopefully demonstrated throughout this book, the earth is full of intelligent, caring and insanely interesting people you can pass time with, I highly recommend getting out there and finding the people who speak your language, not only literally, but also energetically, subliminally, non-verbally and authentically. These are some of life's greatest treasures and pleasures.

Despite our uniqueness, we're all the same. There are many varieties, for sure, varieties of the same. To deny that is to deny life itself. Every one of us exists only while there is breath in our lungs. From the first breath we draw on our way in, to the last one on our way out, our life is coloured, flavoured and punctuated by the quality of the breaths in between. Our choice is how we live this life and use the potential with which we are gifted.

I encourage you to make time to squelch barefoot through the dew-soaked grasslands of life. Don't be too precious. Make a mess here and there. Make time and space for the simplest of pleasures, for it is in this flawed, unapologetic and unyielding existence that we can fully enjoy and embrace all our undeniably human fallibility.

Chapter Twenty

Fasting Practice

Fasting is a word I was familiar with through my upbringing. I remember in school we used to do a 'sponsored fast' around the time of Lent, which is the forty days before Easter in the Christian calendar. The three-prong focus of Lent is fasting, almsgiving and prayer. Fasting is seen as a practice of abstention, be that from specific foods, meals or other habits. This deliberate choice of conscious abstinence is believed to be conducive to spiritual practices and is even said to deepen the connection to God.

When I was younger, I remember participating in this practice in primary school. We would fast for twelve hours during the day and bring a sponsor sheet home to ask friends and family to donate. I believe that this money was donated to the Trócaire charity. I didn't bring this practice into my teens and twenties; however, throughout my thirties, I came to practice and observe the effects and benefits of fasting across a range of aspects.

When I first returned to fasting as an adult, it was without all the associated religious dogma. I understood it to be a spiritual practice, of course, but I also became aware that many people in the health and fitness industry across the globe championed the benefits of fasting simply from a health maintenance and detox perspective, so I decided to learn some more about it and give it a go. What I have learned about myself, my relationship with food and accessing flow states was really quite revelatory, so I will share some of that with you now. First, however, I will offer caution around eating disorders and say that if you have disordered eating, please liaise with a professional, be that your GP, your therapist or maybe a trusted nutritionist to ensure you have the appropriate support to undertake such practices without risking your health unnecessarily.

When I first began fasting, it was at a very low level. I was breastfeeding at the time, and some of the information I saw on support group pages across social media warned against fasting while breastfeeding, suggesting that it could negatively impact milk production. Since I was at least twelve months into breastfeeding and therefore not the only source of nutrition for my child, I decided to try out a few sixteen to eighteen hour fasts, ensuring that I had plenty of water throughout the day and that the foods I did eat when I broke my fast were appropriate to support milk production. These first few test phases of fasting gave me confidence in what I could comfortably handle, and I couldn't perceive any material impact on my ability to produce milk, so I continued. Again, I will point out at this stage that this is only my experience. Each of us is different, and our bodies may respond differently to the same stimuli. This isn't a manual on how you should go about these things, it's a reflection on how I have experienced them.

Next, I tried a few twenty-four-hour fasts and again was surprised by how comfortably I could manage these. At this point, I was still carrying quite a bit of "baby weight" and was beginning to notice the impact of fasting on stripping away excess fat from my body. I didn't start fasting for longer than that until I was finished breastfeeding, but once I had, I committed to a forty-hour fast once per week, having a final meal on a Sunday evening and not eating again until a Tuesday morning. This is where I noticed the most profound impact of fasting in relation to my spiritual practices and teachings, my resilience and mental fortitude and even on things that I had otherwise struggled with for years.

Let's begin with the menstrual cycle. I used to really struggle with heavy bleeds ever since they started. The cramps would be so intense, they'd be enough to floor me on occasion and while I was still at school aged fifteen to eighteen, I could often be found propped up against a radiator at school during break, lunch and any study lesson whilst on my period. Imagine my surprise when I had my first period in a fasted state and was entirely symptom-free. The weekly practice of fasting meant that it wasn't long until I got to see if that had been a one-off, a fluke, or if the two were related. One month later and I had yet another symptom-free menstruation and at this point, I was feeling two things; gobsmacked that something so simple could have such a drastic effect on my experience and a huge sense of indignity that I had been prescribed hormonal treatment to address the monthly symptoms rather than been educated on potential treatments that might be worth exploring before reverting to a pharmaceutical intervention. It's well established at this point that the world, not least the UK and woefully trailing behind Northern Ireland, has prioritized studying the male anatomy within the world of medicine, and what little we do know about women's health is barely a fraction of what there is to know at this point.

Sure enough, if my period began on the Friday before my weekly fast, and I ate as normal, the symptoms would come back with a vengeance. It seemed to me that my dreadfully painful menstruation symptoms were entirely fuelled and sustained by glucose. Now, some people warn against fasting during your period, and that is all well and good. I am not a nutritionist, and I am not a doctor. I have never researched these things for a PhD, never collected or scrutinized the data that may exist on this subject, and never sought to justify my experience in any way other than to acknowledge the reality of my experience as per my observations.

I feel like this and many other examples in this book point to the nature of contradiction. What is right for one person might not suit another person, but also, there is a significant difference and distinction between aversion caused by the ego and being able to recognise danger cues from the nervous system. Often, these two experiences can feel quite similar in the body and even interplay with each other, which is why mindfulness is such a powerful practice. In the first instance, it gives us the confidence not to react in panic without an appropriate degree of oversight and understanding. It also enables us to access clarity about where our cues are coming from and affords us the space to interrogate how accurate our interpretations of the cues are away from the constructs of what other people insist we believe.

One of the other documented benefits of extended fasting, which is generally considered anything from twenty-four-plus hours, is the body's process of autophagy. That is to say, when the body has had a clear twenty-four hours from the last meal and has switched from processing the consumed glucose generated from food consumption to using stored fat as fuel, the body can then dedicate a significant proportion of its energy or focus on healing. Autophagy, specifically, is a process where the body locates damaged or dangerous cells and proteins, then recycles and regenerates them. For this reason, fasting is also said by many to help reverse the ageing process.

With all this knowledge, you would think that I look half my age, sit well within my recommended BMI, and never eat during the first two days of my period. However, one of the other things I have learned through fasting is how emotionally reliant I am on food. You might not be surprised to hear that, as I have highlighted (several times at this point) my complicated relationship with food. When stress levels are high, or I am not conscious of how, what and when I consume, I eat around the clock. I saw this through various sleep regressions where tiredness would have me reaching for anything for breakfast and mindlessly grazing throughout the day until bedtime. I saw it with other significant life events since, and I think it is worth noting, as I had mentioned before, that context is everything. If I am fasting and it feels like a punishment, like really hard work, I'm not convinced this is the practice either because I'm generating Sankhāra, right? Aversion to the practice. This is not something to deliberately rehearse.

Better to practice the right things when we feel adequately resourced than to push through punishing routines in the hope of progress. I am all about the path of least resistance, and as I head into my forties, I've realised that what once worked for me may not necessarily apply indefinitely as my body once again undertakes yet another substantial transformation process. At this stage in my life, my modus operandi is to listen to my body, understand my needs and advocate for myself authentically.

And what of fasting as a spiritual practice? Well, first of all, I want to touch on some of what I learned through my yoga teacher training. We had a London-based teacher called Shiv Sharma, an incredibly talented and respected yoga teacher and physicist, who would occasionally come and deliver weekend seminars as part of our training programme. We studied how to leverage knowledge of anatomy and physics to improve our personal practice and wisdom as teachers. We would frequently deconstruct poses and focus on one specific joint function within an otherwise quite complex yoga pose. When I would ask questions about what other limbs and joints should be doing at the same time, he would say, "Just focus on this." It was a difficult practice to begin with, but when part of it made sense, it all made sense. We would be instructed to drop all the other tension in our bodies and only work with the effort we needed for a specific purpose. Eventually, this cue was distilled down to "only work with 20% effort, maximum," and I believe this specific change to my practice is what revolutionized my entire understanding of how our bodies operate. I remember asking Shiv what his understanding was of the relationship between fasting and a movement-based practice. What was it that fuelled a movement-based practice if it wasn't food? This is where I was first introduced to the idea of muscles being fuelled by the breath. Essentially, Shiv described that working below 20% effort allows us to engage the muscles, which are fuelled by the breath. Anything above that, and we activate the muscles, which are fuelled by glucose. When we work with the muscles fuelled by the breath, we should be able to sustain this work indefinitely since we can access an infinite reservoir of fuel, as conversely is not the case with glucose fuel. As he explained this to me, I recalled what I had learned about fast-twitch and slow-twitch muscles in my sports and fitness studies many years before. I was familiar with the concept that high-energy movement requires explosive power and quick reactions. Sprinting, pitch-based team sports and the world of weightlifting, for example, rely heavily on the fast-twitch muscle body and prioritise glucose as fuel. In the competitive arena, there are strict protocols on what and when to eat for maximum impact, which also extends to regulation around weight categories and other areas. Yoga, however, does not require fast-twitch muscle activation and needn't be practised as such. Now, I don't know about modern-day schools of yoga, though I suspect some of the more contemporary iterations of a yoga practice might lean more towards fast than slow twitch.

So that's how I came to understand how the body can sustain movement and even general day-to-day activity while in a fasted state. Until that point, from all the content I had understood and consumed online, the recurring advice was to temper fast days with less work and general output for health and safety reasons, with little or no speculation on the body's ability to pursue or even excel at particular things while fasting. I began referring to the muscles we use for movement while fasting as 'spirit muscles,' and certainly, the more I understand what it is to maintain a fasting practice and a conscious awareness of what we consume more broadly, the more I relate to this name for them. Working with these muscles enables us to move away from feelings of insecurity, inadequacy or insufficiency to feelings of empowerment, fortitude and gratitude.

In my training diary from when I broke my ankle, I observed these two muscle bodies, one on each side of my body, in real-time as they developed to accommodate what my body was going through. Within the first two weeks of my recovery from injury, my right thigh had grown two inches in circumference simply from all the load-bearing it was doing. Each time I took to my crutches and travelled across a room or space, or trained a movement practice relying only on my right leg, my body signalled to my muscles that we needed more fast-twitch fibres to support the more than doubled workload of the right thigh. I was surprised to see how quickly my body adapted to supporting all my weight on one limb and I marvelled once more at just how responsive our bodies are in adapting to change. What was more surprising was my observations about how my injured leg was operating. Any time I wasn't resting my left leg, I used breathwork to manage muscle tension, both to keep the foot elevated away from the floor and to prevent the muscles from contracting due to habitual mindlessness. When doing a simple drill lying on the floor in about week three, the drill was an alternate side leg raise, i.e. not both sides simultaneously, rather one leg for several reps, then the other. I was surprised to notice a significant difference in the speed at which my left leg would move compared to my right. My left leg felt abnormally light; movement was effortless, and it required me to recalibrate how much effort that limb required to do the work – like when you go to pick something up and it's much lighter than you expected, that's how it felt. Conversely, the right leg felt remarkably heavier, slower and undoubtedly less coordinated. I was genuinely surprised to observe the difference between the two, and it's not a distinction I went looking for – it was just there, crystal clear through the practice. Learning to work with the spirit muscles, as I understand it, can make us infinitely lighter and more agile and, at the same time, be more sustainable than relying solely on food as the fuel for movement.

One other observable impact was something I saw teaching yoga and meditation while fasting. I wouldn't generally inform my students that I was fasting in my initial stages of exploration and yet, my students would consistently comment on the classes I taught while in a fasted state, conveying how they had been so moved in that particular lesson, felt more connected or were able to access deeper states of relaxation. There was something I experienced around the clarity of intention and instruction which was available to them when I taught in a fasted state, and this again suggested to me how one could perceive a closeness to God, or universal oneness – however you might choose to describe it - through a fasting practice.

Slight detour: one of the things I teach that people are often surprised to learn (or remember) is that the respiratory system is one of the body's excretory systems. It removes and replaces stale air from the lungs and offloads gases and other waste products generated through cell respiration. Much like our digestive system, our respiratory system brings in resources, extracts the beneficial elements we require for our health and excretes remnants as by-products. While these systems have very different organs and appear concerned with distinctly different processes, they are surprisingly similar in some ways. With so much knowledge and education available these days, we assume to know how the body and everything else works, often missing out on the subtleties of automated physiological operations; however, if we can sit quietly and listen, we can discover things that generally aren't discussed in mainstream discourse. Personally, I would argue that being in a fasted state highlights the power of love as a source of fuel. Given that we are such social animals, I don't think this is such a stretch, and I'll explain why.

In practising fasting and mindfulness, I have noticed almost accidentally the times that I have fasted without trying. When I say that I am an emotional eater, it is always quite interesting for me to notice when I do not feel the need to consume, especially if I'm in the company of other people. What I have come to observe is that there are places and people with whom fasting is effortless, and there are situations and scenarios where it feels like the only way through is with food. I believe that this is another reason why many people report feeling more connected to God when fasting. In my experience, I have witnessed a global sensation of peace and contentedness when I can comfortably abstain from food, even when others in my company are not. I think something we've really lost sight of in the modern day is how critical our sense of connection is, be that to each other, to ourselves or to something greater, and how that relates to our perception of feeling nourished. We know how important healthy attachment is to our development in those most formative first few years, and we've all heard of an elderly couple where one has died of a broken heart within weeks of losing the other. Love is nourishment, and I believe it should be regarded as equally essential to our health and vitality as any balanced diet or movement practice throughout our lifetime, not just our infancy.

As an extension to this, let's take a moment to consider a fasting approach in relation to other things we consume beyond the digestive system. I believe we need to reframe how we prioritise what's important in life. When we mindlessly consume things which elevate our heart rate and bring tension into the muscles by triggering a stress response in our nervous system, which is frequently accompanied by a plethora of sub-conscious breath holds, I would argue that we are mentally, physically, emotionally and spiritually exhausting ourselves by stealth.

Resetting our baseline of anxiety higher and higher so that we continue to crave more excessive and extreme content. This becomes a vicious cycle, and I fear it's one of our most dangerous cultural norms of the 21st century, underpinned by unregulated social media platforms and even through the mainstream TV and film productions we consume. From the sensory assault of HD images, flashing lights and stereo surround sound to the carefully curated sales copy which seeks to profit from your mindless conditioning, we are at the mercy of people who have educated themselves in the art of manipulation to ensure the growth of their bottom line. I have seen a practice like fasting, coupled with meditation, empower me to not react to these subtle, pervasive cues which are littered throughout our day. I frequently fast from 'social' media. As mentioned at the beginning, I have learned to abstain from feverishly responding and reacting to everything that appears in my many inboxes. Much like thoughts in a meditation practice, not every notification on my phone is worthy of my attention or reaction. When we strip away all the excess, we realise how little we need to survive and thrive.

Chapter Twenty-One

Find Your Frequency

When people first meet me, they think I'm nice, friendly, good company, fun, affectionate, interesting and so on. They think I have an effortlessly sunny disposition. At the risk of sounding like a bit of a knob, they think they've found someone who is just completely on their wavelength. At times, dare I say it, some might even think they have found their soul mate. This is how estranged many of us are from the frequency or feeling of unconditional love.

What they don't see are the years of painstaking work, self-excavation and personal enquiry I've undertaken. They misinterpret my dedication to intentionally cultivating equanimity when faced with difficult situations as just being laid back by nature. *"I'm so lucky to be that way."* It reminds me of a cartoon I saw that illustrates a conversation between an artist and an onlooker.

The onlooker says "Oh, I wish I could do that" and the artist replies "It's just practice" and the onlooker says "You're so lucky to have this innate talent" and the artist says "It's practice" and the onlooker, in total rejection of the idea that dedicating one's life to skills acquisition and playful exploration could enable them to develop such a high level of proficiency, says once more "I suppose you were born with this talent" and the artist gives up trying to explain because clearly this commentator is not in a position to hear anything that runs contrary to their own self-limiting beliefs. Each one of us has innate qualities and talents, but we shouldn't underestimate the potential and impact that comes from consistency of practice and a willingness to show up.

Through this work, and over and over again throughout my studies, I have repeatedly come across the same frequency. We know light has a frequency, and we know sound has a frequency. I would also argue that love has a frequency, that universal consciousness has a frequency and that practices have frequencies. Heck, physics teaches us that even solid, inanimate objects like hardwood tables and concrete blocks have a frequency. So when we explore the realm of energetics, we need to be open-minded, of course, but we also need to recognize that much of what we understand and demonstrate from a physics perspective is only really the tip of the iceberg. I suspect we'll have huge breakthroughs on the horizon in this field particularly over the coming years. One of the things I always found peculiar about people backing their arguments with science and arguing that it can be the only explanation is that they fail to acknowledge that science, by its very nature, tests what it knows. The point of the test? To discover if what we think we know holds up to scrutiny. When science learns more, it unashamedly changes what it says. We could learn a lot from this fluid understanding and openness to receive more data, which might ultimately change our whole perspective.

Through my sound therapy studies, I learned about concepts such as *entrainment* and *sympathetic resonance.* Entrainment is described generally as a process of synchronizing *things*, and in sound therapy specifically, we talk about the less dominant frequency or frequencies entraining to the dominant one. When I learned about this, it reminded me of my time spent in the compound in Sri Lanka on my Vipassana retreat and explained for me how others seemed to fall into my frequency, matching habitual patterns like the cadence of my walk and so on, but we can even witness this through simple things like an audience clapping along to live music. We can hear when an audience gets involved in a performance by clapping in time to the music. To me, the observable difference between whether that clapping accompaniment stays on rhythm or not is the dominant frequency. So, if the dominant frequency is an audience member who is really keen and clapping but has zero capacity to keep in time with the music, the audience can get carried away with the clapping regardless of what rhythm the music is playing. Conversely, when the audience claps along to the music and stays in time with the music, this is because the dominant frequency, which everyone else is entrained to, is in time, and the dominant frequency might come from the rhythm section of the band, or it might come from someone in the audience. It can be from anywhere.

This idea of entraining rhythms is important since our heart is essentially a living drumbeat. You can observe the effects of entrainment within your own body by playing very fast heavy metal or drum and bass while observing your heart rate versus your heart rate when listening to soothing classical or meditation music. It is even more obvious when we observe how we drive faster when listening to high-energy pop music versus listening to an audiobook, for example. What we consume, even aurally, impacts our muscle tension, which affects the symptoms. Speeding in your vehicle might not be your intention, but it can certainly be a symptom of what's happening subconsciously, depending on your environment. Once we understand how external influences can have such a drastic influence and impact on our physiology, we can begin to understand our own power and potential to direct that through conscious awareness.

Sympathetic resonance is another impressive phenomenon we can observe in group singing contexts. An example could be how someone is singing slightly out of key until they hear the correct pitch, which they then match. Similarly, if you've never learned to sing in harmony, in the beginning, you might find that you sing your line perfectly until the harmony line is added, at which point you end up in sympathetic resonance with the harmony line rather than your own. This is demonstrable in controlled settings using two tuning forks of the same pitch. When two folks of the same or similar enough frequency are in proximity and one is struck, the other will also begin to vibrate. Incidentally, this would not be the case if the forks were different pitches to begin with.

These two principles of sound therapy demonstrate how we can not only curate our own frequency but we can also deliberately cultivate it and share it with others. The best way to ensure that yours is the dominant frequency in any situation is to train your frequency through a dedicated practice. That way, you'll be very grounded in your own frequency, but you will also be less susceptible to the influence of other frequencies.

I believe that spirituality or faith and flow states are the same frequency. They require an element of surrender, and they rely on an ability to connect to something beyond ourselves. I remember being triggered quite a bit in my early yoga teacher training days by a variety of things I had to confront in myself. And yet, I managed to stay the course. There was something familiar and comforting about being held in that safe space as I found my bearings and orientated myself towards my own potential while systematically reviewing my biases. I recognised the frequency of non-judgement and equanimity and could identify it more easily each time I encountered it since.

On this path, you may come across people who insist that their needs are more important than yours. You may even learn to recognize this frequency before any verbal engagement with them. I have been surprised at some of the situations I have found myself in, most often when I have withdrawn from engagement to stay true to my own practices and needs. Often, this vacuum is enough to elicit aggravated demands such as the one above. It's much like I pointed out in the beginning about being a vegetarian and how very often people I interacted with were determined to take it as a personal slight to them rather than an acknowledgement of my own personal preferences and needs. When you hear this opinion articulated in response to your decisions, conduct or boundaries, I encourage you to take a few calming, cleansing breaths, in through the nose, out through the mouth with as little tension as possible. Remember, 20% effort, maximum. Try not to get swept up into a reactionary need to "be a good (whatever)," or to validate anyone else. As I had to learn more than once already, you are allowed to put yourself first. It is right that you regard yourself with the reverence of the remarkable being that you are.

Likewise, other people may try to impose their notion of what is good for you on you. I, at one time, misunderstood that any form of movement meditation was essentially cheating as this seemed to be what was communicated through the rules of engagement on the Vipassana retreat. When I tried to use my years of meditation experience to navigate the realm of self-defence, I soon learned that movement meditation can be at least equally as challenging as any seated practice, offering at least as many opportunities for learning and growth.

The antidote to modern-day, stress-based illness is creativity and expression. Arts practices are generally quite meditative by nature. I would argue that we can access many of the benefits of meditation without ever undertaking a formal, seated practice. For Skinner, swimming is his meditation. For someone else, it might be singing, running, painting, dancing, juggling, praying, being in nature, or being in community. There are many ways to access these states once we recognise that they all have the same frequency and lay down expectations of what any particular practice should look like. In finding my frequency, I've led group singing projects, performed solo on stages of various sizes, recorded my own original music and produced an international collaboration album. I've performed with fire and LED props, participated in artists' residencies, created textile installations, run an online festival and now, published a book. Your potential is greater than you could ever imagine and limited only by your belief in yourself.

It's all the same frequency; don't pursue it fanatically or try to hoard it. Much like the elusive stringed quartet I could hear during my Vipassana experience, such attempts will likely only curtail your sensitivity and dull your senses; as is the nature of the relationship between creativity and tension.

These days, you might notice that a lot of the business and leadership jargon uses mindfulness-based phrases, terminology and concepts, albeit with a slightly different accent on the language used. It is often deployed to describe how to increase business awareness within the context of change and transformation and how to use emotional intelligence to manage teams and mitigate conflict.

These simple principles of understanding that we have more embodied wisdom than we can really evidence or articulate fully at this point will be the key in navigating what is deemed these days to be a VUCA (Volatile, Uncertain, Complex and Ambiguous) world. We have never needed enduring patience, small egos, big hearts and unadulterated creativity more than we do now. Learn what your ideal frequency feels like and how to recognize it. Learn how to cultivate it and how to share it.

Find your frequency.

About the Author

Róisín is a natural-born facilitator and guide who loves nothing more than to study and share practices which explore the many facets of *The Art of Being Human,* for contentedness and wellbeing. She is passionate about designing accessible ways for groups and individuals to find their entry point, their frequency.

If she's not at home enjoying the quiet life, you can find her traipsing barefoot through a forest or festival.

She is an avid traveller and life-long student.

With a background in circus arts and festivals, she is adept at project management and production.

To others, she is a mother, wife, daughter, sister, friend and teacher.

www.roisinerskine.com